Achieve Level 5-6

English
Revision and Practice
Key Stage 3

Marie Lallaway, Tom Johns and Mig Bennett

Rising★Stars

PLEASE NOTE: THIS BOOK MAY NOT BE PHOTOCOPIED OR REPRODUCED AND WE APPRECIATE YOUR HELP IN PROTECTING OUR COPYRIGHT.

Rising Stars UK Ltd, 22 Grafton Street, London W1S 4EX

www.risingstars-uk.com

Published 2008

Text, design and layout © 2008 Rising Stars UK Ltd.

Editorial: Sandra Stafford
Illustrations: Phill Burrows
Design: Branford Graphics
Cover design: Words & Pictures Ltd

Acknowledgements
p10–11 Extracts from *Ray Mears Bushcraft Survival* by Ray Mears;
p14 Extract from *The Kite Rider* by Geraldine McCaughrean, Oxford University Press;
p18 'How your money helps' www.oxfam.org.uk;
p20 Extract from *Spilled Water* by Sally Grindley, Bloomsbury;
p21 Extract from *Powder Monkey* by Paul Dowsell, Bloomsbury;
p22 Extract from *Great Expectations* by Charles Dickens;
p23 Extract from *Frankenstein* by Mary Shelley;
p24 Extract from *Animal Farm* by George Orwell;
p25 'How to invest in collectible toys' www.timesonline.co.uk;
p26 *Boy* by Roald Dahl. Reproduced by permission of Jonathan Cape Ltd & Penguin Books Ltd.;
p28–29 Extracts from *The Other Side of the Dale* by Gervase Phinn;
p30 Extract from *The Kite Runner* by Khaled Hosseini, Bloomsbury;
p32 Extract from *Chewing the Cud* by Dick King-Smith;
p34 Extract from *The Eagle of the Ninth* by Rosemary Sutcliffe.

Picture acknowledgements
p9 Rob Cousins/Alamy; p10 Kevin Arnold/The Image Bank/Getty Images;
p12 Suzann Julien/iStockphoto.com; p22 BFI; p23 Sygma/Corbis;
p25 Steve Gorton/Dorling Kindersley/Getty Images; p34 Bettmann/CORBIS; p36 Carol Buchanan/Dreamstime.com; p59 Lodge Photo/Mathew Lodge/Alamy.

All rights reserved. No part of this publication may be reproduced, stored in a retrieval system, or transmitted, in any form by any means, electronic, mechanical, photocopying, recording or otherwise, without the prior permission of Rising Stars.

British Library Cataloguing in Publication Data.
A CIP record for this book is available from the British Library.

ISBN: 978 1 84680 470 0

Printed by Craft Print International Ltd, Singapore

Contents

How to use this book	4
About the Key Stage 3 National Tests in English	8
Introduction to reading skills	9
Finding information and evidence in a text	10
What does the writer mean but not tell you directly?	14
Commenting on the organisation of a text	18
Commenting on how a writer uses language for effect	22
Understanding the writer's viewpoint and the overall effect of the text	26
Test yourself: practice reading tests	30
Introduction to writing skills	38
Using a wider range of connectives	40
Adding detail with adjectives	42
Adding detail with adverbial phrases	44
Using a full range of punctuation	46
Improve the organisation of your writing	48
Improve your informative writing	50
Improve your persuasive writing	52
Improve your imaginative writing	54
Improve your writing to review	56
How to tackle the writing task	58
Test yourself: practice writing tasks	59
Self-assessment sheet	61
Answers	62

LEVEL 5–6

How to use this book

This book offers you advice about how to improve your reading and writing skills. We know that students **learn by doing** so practice is an important part of the book. It is designed to help you progress towards the next level and do your best in the Key 3 Stage National Tests.

The reading skills section (pages 10–29) and writing skills section (pages 38–57) have the following features to make them easy to use and highlight what you really need to be able to do.

1. **Target level statement** – This tells you what you need to do to move towards the next level in each of the key reading and writing skills. The target level is shown in bold.

2. **Assessment focus** – The main reading or writing skill that is being practised to help you prepare for the National Tests. See pages 6 and 7 for more information.

3. **Tips** – Each page includes tips to remind you of key points that will help you to succeed at a skill.

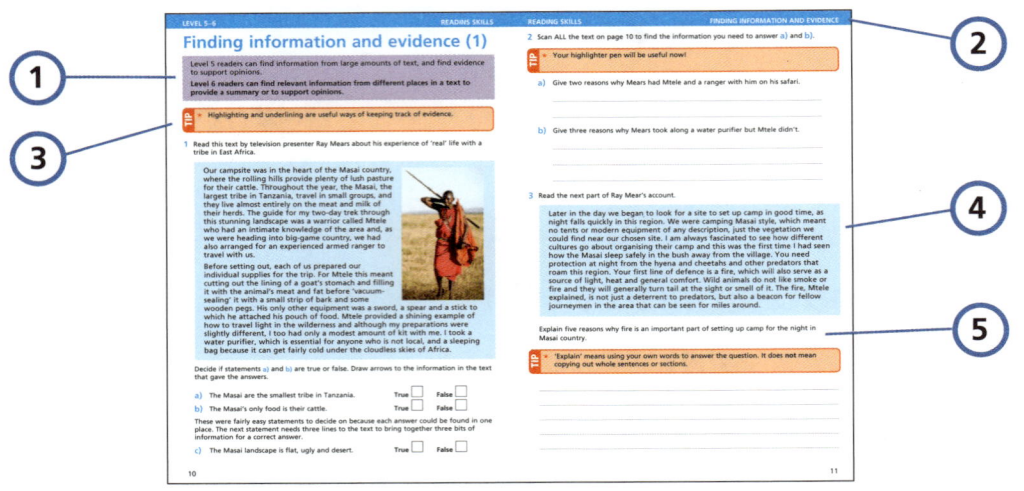

Example Reading skills page

4. **Text example** – Lots of fiction and non-fiction examples for you to work through.

5. **Practice questions** – Varied exercises help you to practise skills that will help you to improve your reading and writing – both in class and in the National Tests.

   Answers to the practice questions are provided at the back of the book (pages 62–64).

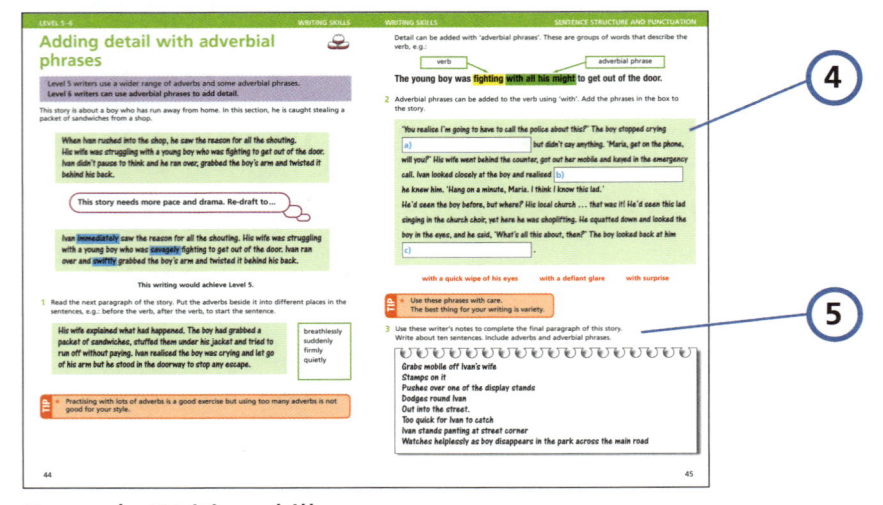

Example Writing skills page

4

LEVEL 5–6

HOW TO USE THIS BOOK

Practice tests

Mini-reading tests (pages 30–37):
Use these tests to practise your reading skills on a longer text extract. The questions are similar in style to those in the National Tests. Each test includes two text extracts and a series of 1, 2, 3 and 5 mark questions. The assessment focus for each question is given to help you identify the key skill you need to answer it. Answers are provided at the end of the book.

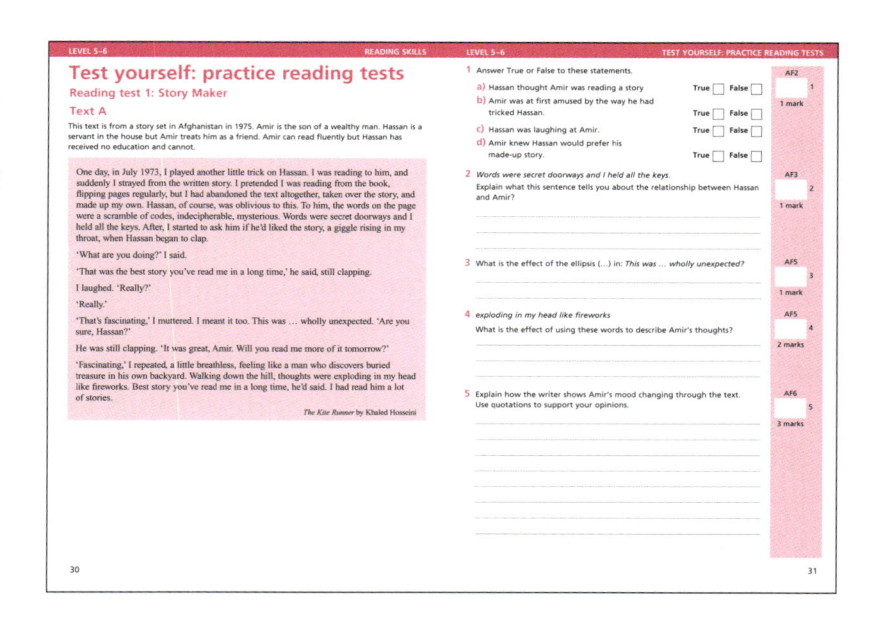

Writing tasks (pages 59–60):
Use the two National Test-style writing tasks to practise your writing skills on a longer piece of writing. A planning sheet accompanies the longer writing task (page 60). Use it to help you plan your writing and organise your answer before you begin to write it in full.

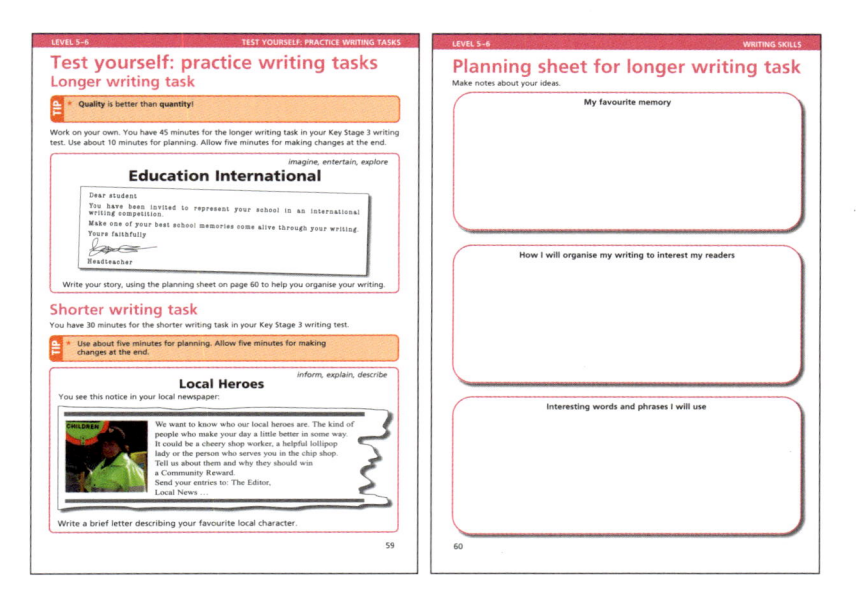

Writing self-assessment sheet (page 61):
See page 61 to identify the level at which you are writing. Find examples in your answer to the shorter and longer writing tasks and highlight them on the grid. When you have highlighted at least 10 of the descriptions for a level it means you have achieved it! Highlight in a different colour the areas you need to improve.

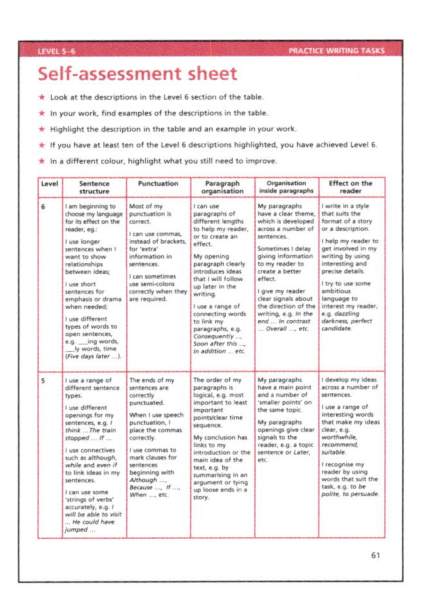

LEVEL 5–6 HOW TO USE THIS BOOK

Reading skills

The Key Stage 3 National Tests assess your reading skills in the following areas.

> ★ **AF2:** Understand, describe, select or retrieve information, events or ideas from texts and use quotation and reference to text.
>
> ★ **AF3:** Deduce, infer or interpret information, events or ideas from texts.
>
> ★ **AF4:** Identify and comment on the structure and organisation of texts, including grammatical and presentational features at text level.
>
> ★ **AF5:** Explain and comment on writers' use of language, including grammatical and literary features at word and sentence level.
>
> ★ **AF6:** Identify and comment on writers' purposes and viewpoints and the overall effect of the text on the reader.

Each AF (assessment focus) describes a different set of reading skills.
In this book you will actively revise, practise and improve your ability to do the following.

> **AF2:** Find information and evidence in a text (pages 10–13). 
>
> **AF3:** Understand what the writer means but does not tell you directly (pages 14–17). 
>
> **AF4:** Comment on the organisation of texts (pages 18–21). 
>
> **AF5:** Comment on how a writer uses language for effect (pages 22–25). 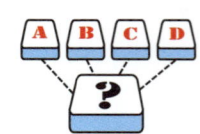
>
> **AF6:** Understand the writer's viewpoint and the overall effect of the text (pages 26–29).

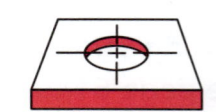

✓ Each section targets a different skill and practises the skill in a variety of ways that will help you to develop your understanding of reading in any situation, including for the National Tests.

✓ Each section gives you practice at working with both fiction and non-fiction texts. These include examples of print-based and electronic (e.g. Internet) texts.

✓ Finally, there are two 'mini' Key Stage 3 National Test-style reading tests for you to check how well your revision is going.

Writing skills

The Key Stage 3 National Tests assess your writing skills in the following areas.

In the KS3 National Tests you will be assessed on your ability to do these things.

- ★ **AF1:** Write imaginative, interesting and thoughtful texts.
- ★ **AF2:** Produce texts which are appropriate to task, reader and purpose.
- ★ **AF3:** Organise and present whole texts effectively, sequencing and structuring information, ideas and events.
- ★ **AF4:** Construct paragraphs and use cohesion within and between paragraphs.
- ★ **AF5:** Vary sentences for clarity, purpose and effect.
- ★ **AF6:** Write with technical accuracy of syntax and punctuation in phrases, clauses and sentences.
- ★ **AF7:** Select appropriate and effective vocabulary.

Each assessment focus describes a different feature of writing.

In this book, you will revise, practise and improve your ability to do the following.

AF5/6/7: Construct complex sentences, including use of connectives, adjectives, adverbs, and punctuation (pages 40–47).

AF3/4: Organise your writing, focusing on the use of paragraph and text organisation devises (pages 48–49).

AF1/2: Use an appropriate style for the task and reader (pages 50–57).

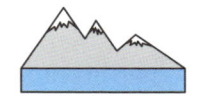

✓ At the end of the book there are two National Test-style writing tasks – one shorter and one longer. Use these to practise writing the sort of text you might have to write in your KS3 writing test.

✓ Use the self-assessment sheet on page 61 to check what level you are writing at and see what you need to do to improve.

✓ Each section targets a different skill and practises that skill in a variety of ways to help you to develop your ability to write in any situation, including for the National Tests.

Use the book to work on the skills you know you need to practise. Or, work through the whole book for overall improvement.

LEVEL 5–6

About the Key Stage 3 National Tests in English

You will take three tests in English: the Reading paper, the Shakespeare paper and the Writing paper. These are designed to test your reading and writing skills.

★ **The Reading test:** This test assesses your reading comprehension. It lasts for 1 hour and 15 minutes. You have the first 15 minutes to read the paper but you cannot open the writing paper until this time is up. You then have 1 hour to answer the questions. Begin by skimming through all the questions. Refer closely to the texts when answering the questions and use evidence from the text to back up questions when you are asked to.

★ **The Writing test:** There are two writing tasks – one shorter (30 minutes long) and one longer (45 minutes long). Remember to keep your handwriting neat for these tasks to help the examiner mark your paper.

★ **The longer writing task** is a test of extended writing. There is a planning sheet for use with it – use this to make notes and organise your writing. You have 15 minutes' planning time. You must complete this task before starting the shorter writing task. Spelling is not assessed in this task.

★ **The shorter writing task** is a test of your ability to write concisely. Spelling is assessed in this task.

★ **The Shakespeare paper:** This paper is 45 minutes long and includes two extracts from the play you have studied in class. This paper assesses your reading skills, not writing. This book does not cover the Shakespeare paper.

Test techniques

Before the test

1. Revise 'little and often' rather than in long sessions. It is easier to concentrate for a short period of time and you will remember more.
2. Read the tips throughout the book to remind you of important points.
3. Revise with a friend. You can encourage and learn from each other.
4. Be prepared – bring your own pens and pencils with you to the test.

During the test

1. Read the questions carefully, then read them again!
2. Underline key words in the question.
3. If you get stuck, don't stay on the same question – move on! You can come back to it later.
4. Never leave a multiple-choice question unanswered. Make an educated guess if you really can't work out the answer.
5. Check to see how many marks each question is worth. Have you 'earned' those marks with your answer?
6. Check your answers after each question. Does your answer look correct?

LEVEL 5–6

Introduction to reading skills

The idea of reading 'skills' may seem an odd idea. After all, you have probably been 'reading' since you were about five years old and can 'read' most of the words you see.

People generally think that 'reading' questions ask you to find information in a text. Some do, but there are other ways in which a person 'reads' a text. Understanding and improving these skills will help you to:

★ get more pleasure from your reading;

★ answer questions in the Key Stage 3 National Tests.

Working with a reading text is a bit like being an archaeologist making a fascinating discovery. You don't see everything at first sight.

Reading skills help you to find the interesting details below the surface of a text.

In this book we focus on developing and practising the following reading skills.

★ Finding information and evidence in a text (pages 10–13)

★ Understanding what the writer means but does not tell you directly (pages 14–17)

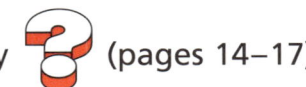

★ Commenting on the organisation of a text (pages 18–21)

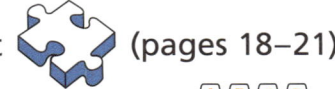

★ Commenting on how a writer uses language for effect (pages 22–25)

★ Understanding the writer's viewpoint and the overall effect of the text (pages 26–29)

Read the information, do the tasks and check your answers to become a Level 6 reader.

9

LEVEL 5–6 | READING SKILLS

Finding information and evidence in a text (1)

Level 5 readers can find information from large amounts of text, and find evidence to support opinions.

Level 6 readers can find relevant information from different places in a text to provide a summary or to support opinions.

TIP ★ Highlighting and underlining are useful ways of keeping track of evidence.

1 Read this text by television presenter Ray Mears about his experience of 'real' life with a tribe in East Africa.

> Our campsite was in the heart of Masai country, where the rolling hills provide plenty of lush pasture for their cattle. Throughout the year, the Masai, the largest tribe in Tanzania, travel in small groups, and they live almost entirely on the meat and milk of their herds. The guide for my two-day trek through this stunning landscape was a warrior called Mtele, who had an intimate knowledge of the area, and as we were heading into big-game country, we had also arranged for an experienced, armed ranger to travel with us.
>
> Before setting out, each of us prepared our individual supplies for the trip. For Mtele this meant cutting out the lining of a goat's stomach and filling it with the animal's meat and fat before 'vacuum-sealing' it with a small strip of bark and some wooden pegs. His only other equipment was a sword, a spear and a stick to which he attached his pouch of food. Mtele provided a shining example of how to travel light in the wilderness and although my preparations were slightly different, I too had only a modest amount of kit with me in addition to my ready-prepared rations. I also took a water purifier, which is essential for anyone who is not local, and a sleeping bag because it can get fairly cold under the cloudless skies of Africa.
>
> *Ray Mears Bushcraft Survival* by Ray Mears

Decide if statements **a)** and **b)** are True or False. Draw arrows to the information in the text that gave the answers.

a) The Masai are the smallest tribe in Tanzania.   True ☐   False ☐

b) The Masai's only food is their cattle.   True ☐   False ☐

These were fairly easy statements to decide on because each answer could be found in one place. The next statement needs three lines to the text to bring together three bits of information for a correct answer.

c) The Masai landscape is flat, ugly and desert.   True ☐   False ☐

10

LEVEL 5–6   FINDING INFORMATION AND EVIDENCE IN A TEXT

2 Scan ALL the text on page 10 to find the information you need to answer **a)** and **b)**.

> **TIP** ★ Your highlighter pen will be useful now!

a) Give two reasons why Mears had Mtele and a ranger with him on his safari.

_____

_____

b) Give three reasons why Mears took along a water purifier but Mtele didn't.

_____

_____

_____

3 Read the next part of Ray Mears' account.

> Later in the day we began to look for a site to set up camp in good time as night falls quickly in this region. We were camping Masai style which meant no tents or modern equipment of any description, just the vegetation we could find near our chosen site. I am always fascinated to see how different cultures go about organising their camp and this was the first time I had seen how the Masai sleep safely in the bush away from the village. You need protection at night from the hyenas and cheetahs, and other predators that roam this region. Your first line of defence is a fire, which will also serve as a source of heat, light and general comfort. Wild animals do not like smoke or fire and they will generally tend to turn tail at the sight or smell of it. The fire, Mtele explained, is not just a deterrent to predators, but also a beacon for fellow journeymen in the area which can be seen for miles around.
>
> *Ray Mears Bushcraft Survival* by Ray Mears

Explain five reasons why fire is an important part of setting up camp for the night in Masai country.

> **TIP** ★ 'Explain' means using your own words to answer the question. It does **not** mean copying out whole sentences or sections.

_____

_____

_____

_____

_____

11

LEVEL 5–6　　　　　　　　　　　　　　　　　　　　　　　　READING SKILLS

Finding information and evidence in a text (2)

1 Walking and camping in the territory of the American Black Bear is popular but dangerous. Read the advice about how to camp safely in bear territory.

> **TIP** ★ Read the text first, then think about the question. Go back to the text to pick out the information you need.

Don't pitch your tents near bear food sources (fruit bushes or trees, rubbish dumps, dead animals) or where you can see bear tracks or bear claw marks on trees.

Pitch tents in a line or semi-circle. That makes a bear easier to spot if it wanders into the site and gives it an easy escape route.

Don't cook, eat or store food (including chocolate, sweets or their wrappers) in or close to your tents. Avoid using canned foods with strong odours (e.g. tuna, sardines). Wash out any food cans after use.

Keep food in bear-resistant storage containers. Always store food away from the camp.

2 Look at diagrams **A–C**. Tick the camp site that has been set up correctly.

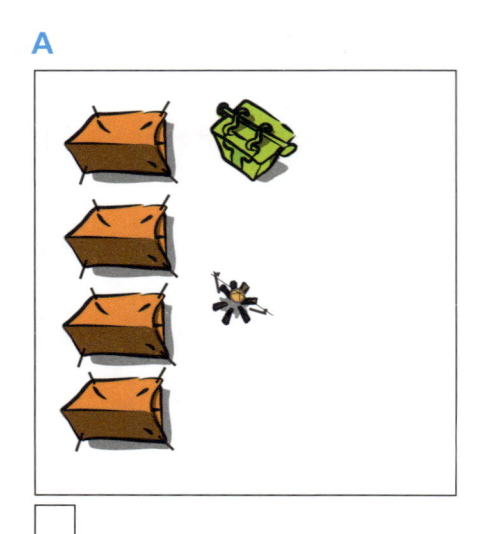

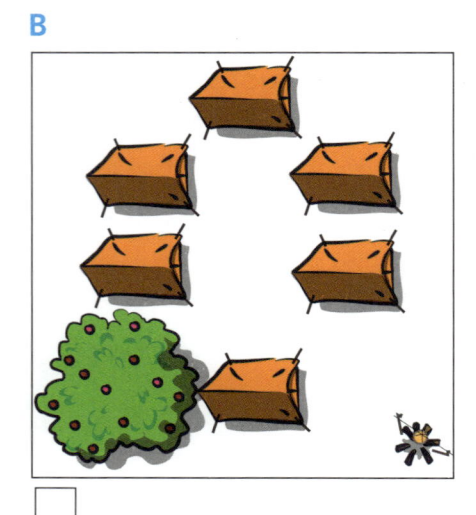

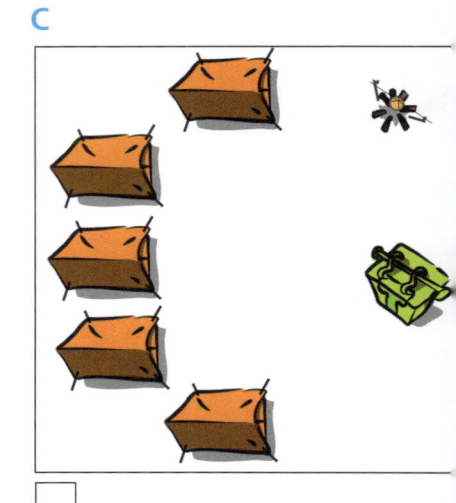

A　　　　　　　　　　B　　　　　　　　　　C

12

LEVEL 5–6   FINDING INFORMATION AND EVIDENCE IN A TEXT

3 There are other ways of trying to keep food away from bears. This diagram gives the correct information.

a) Which instruction (**A** or **B**) gives information that matches the diagram?

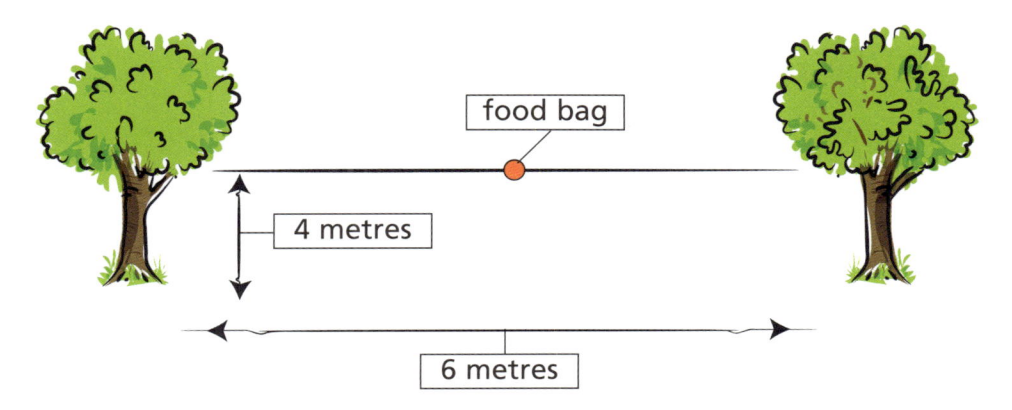

A If you don't have a bear-proof container or vehicle, place food inside several layers of sealed plastic bags (to reduce odour) and put that inside a water-proof bag. If only one tree is available, sling your bag over a branch that is about 4 metres from ground level so that it hangs at least 6 metres from the main trunk. Or, find two trees about 2 metres apart and hang the bag between them at least 4 metres from the ground using nylon cord.

B If you don't have a bear-proof container or vehicle, place food inside several layers of sealed plastic bags (to reduce odour) and put that inside a water-proof bag. If only one tree is available, sling your bag over a branch that is about 4 metres from ground level so that it hangs at least 1.5 metres from the main trunk. Or, find two trees about 6 metres apart and hang the bag between them at least 4 metres from the ground using nylon cord.

b) Read these frequently-asked questions about travelling in bear country. Then match one answer to each question. One has been done for you.

Frequently-asked questions	Answer
1 If a bear stands on its hind legs, is it preparing to charge?	
2 Is a bear's sense of smell better than a dog's?	
3 Are bears naturally aggressive towards humans?	
4 Is running the best way to escape from an aggressive bear?	
5 Does running downhill give you a better chance of escaping from a bear?	A
6 If you walk in bear country, is it best to make a noise to warn off the bears?	

A No. Bears can run faster than any human – in any direction!

B Yes. Bears have one of the most sensitive noses in the animal world.

C No. In that posture a bear is usually trying to identify you by scent or sight.

D No. Bears can run as fast as a racehorse for short distances.

E No. They are shy creatures that only act aggressively when threatened or surprised.

F Yes. That will give it time to move out of your way without feeling threatened.

LEVEL 5–6 READING SKILLS

What does the writer mean but not tell you directly? (1)

Level 5 readers can understand the writer's meanings and explain them in their own words.

Level 6 readers can find deeper meanings in the text and begin to explain them using details to support their answers.

1 Read this story, set in Ancient China. It is about Haoyou, a 12-year-old boy whose father has recently died.

When Haoyou woke, he tried to move so fast that his dream could not cling to him. He determined to shake it off by the sheer speed with which he scuttled out of bed, fetched in the water, brought it to the boil. He concentrated entirely on pouring the hot water into the two cups, without spilling a drop, sprinkling the tea leaves in exactly equal numbers on to the steaming liquid. He spaced two of the cups in the precise centre of the tray, and carried it so carefully that not a single drop spilled. Then he circled the partition to where his parents' bed lay beneath a grey-morning window.

'Good morning, honoured mother and father,' he said, as he had said a thousand times.

Then the tray fell from his hands with a crash, and he stood staring at the shards* of pottery, the spreading puddle of tea. He had been trying so hard to bury his dream under everyday routine that everyday routine had undone him. This was the day after his father's funeral, and he had forgotten his father was dead. 'I'm sorry! I'm sorry! I didn't mean to say it! I forgot! No! I mean I didn't forget. Of course I didn't forget, but . . . .'

His mother sat up, still wearing the clothes of the previous day. It was plain she had not slept. She held out her arms and Haoyou ran to her, like a boat running for harbour in a storm.

shards – broken pieces

The Kite Rider by Geraldine McCaughrean

a) Look at the text highlighted in yellow. Read this Level 5 answer to the question: *How do you know that Haoyou's dream was unpleasant?*

It says he moved 'so fast that his dream could not cling to him'.

★ Does the answer choose the right quotations? Yes ☐ No ☐

★ Does the answer explain how you can tell that Hayou's dream was unpleasant? Yes ☐ No ☐

14

LEVEL 5–6 WHAT DOES THE WRITER MEAN BUT NOT TELL YOU DIRECTLY?

TIP ★ Level 6 answers expect you to explain your thinking using short quotations to support your opinions.

Here's a better answer.

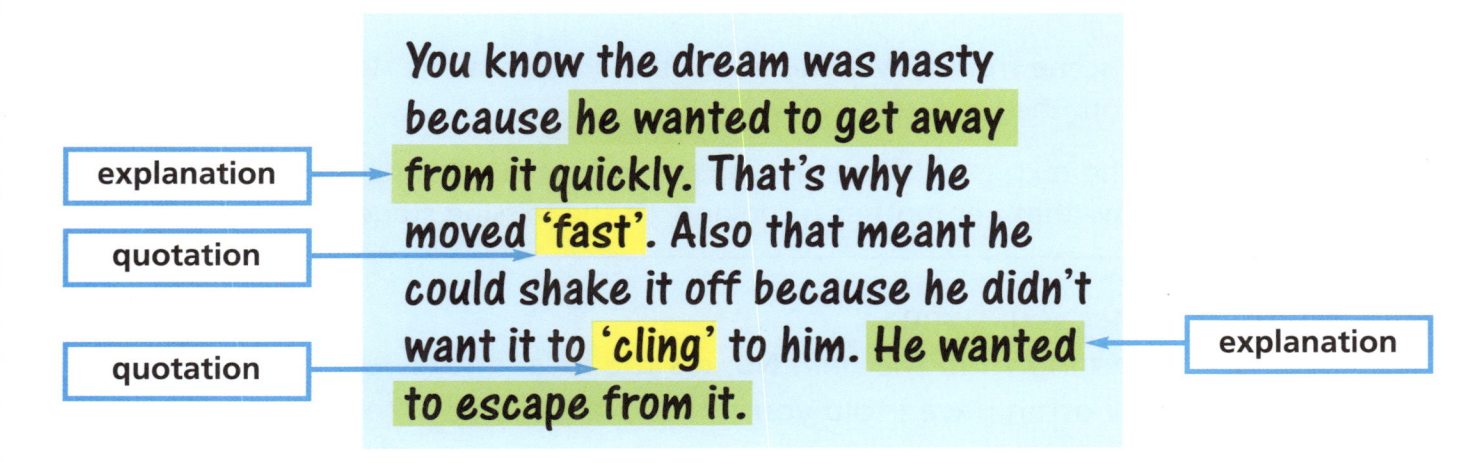

> You know the dream was nasty because **he wanted to get away from it quickly**. That's why he moved '**fast**'. Also that meant he could shake it off because he didn't want it to '**cling**' to him. **He wanted to escape from it.**

[explanation] → "he wanted to get away from it quickly"
[quotation] → 'fast'
[quotation] → 'cling'
[explanation] → "He wanted to escape from it."

2 Look at the text highlighted in blue on page 14. Plan an answer to this question: *Explain what you learn about Haoyou's character from the way he makes the tea.*

  a) Choose two quotations that contain **only** the important words.
  _____
  _____

  b) Consider what they show you about Haoyou.
  _____
  _____

  c) Write up your answer as a paragraph.

3 Look at the text highlighted in green on page 14.
What do you learn about the feelings of Haoyou's mother from this section?

  a) Write a paragraph using the method in question 2 as a guideline.
  b) Using a highlighter, identify the quotations you used in one colour and the explanations in another colour.
  c) Check whether you are 'telling the story'. If so, add another colour.

TIP ★ Telling the story means just repeating the information in the text. Learn to spot 'telling the story' and remove it from your answers.

LEVEL 5–6   READING SKILLS

What does the writer mean but not tell you directly? (2)

Writers often leave things to the reader's imagination, but give **clues** to help.

1 Read the opening scene from a TV series about the Ashton family. Then add the missing stage directions from the list A to F below.

Look for clues in the text, e.g.: 'What are you doing for tea?' Donna must be coming into the kitchen to know that her mother is cooking, so the missing stage direction is **C**.

Mum:	Is that you, Donna?
Donna:	(*shouting from the hall*) No, it's the local nutter.
Mum:	How often have I told you not to slam the door? You'll break the glass one day.
Donna:	[C] Sorry! What are you doing for tea?
Mum:	Beans on toast.
Donna:	[ ] Not again!
Mum:	If you want something different, cook it yourself. I've been at work all day, you know.
Donna:	[ ] No time. Got all this homework to do.
Mum:	Clear that lot out of the way. We need somewhere to eat.
Donna:	Can't I have mine in front of the TV?
Mum:	We eat at the table in this house.
Donna:	[ ] But look it's time for my favourite programme.
Mum:	So what? Get those things off there – now!
Donna:	[ ] Okay, I'm going to my room. Going to get started on my work right now.
Mum:	What about your tea?
Donna:	[ ] Not hungry!
Mum:	What have I told you about slamming doors!

A *Throwing her school bag on the table.* _____
B *Pulls a face.* _____
C *Entering the kitchen.* _____
D *Slams kitchen door on the way out.* _____
E *Pointing at the clock.* _____
F *Picking up her bag.* _____

2 Add an adverb to each stage direction in the list above to show even more understanding of the characters' moods, e.g.: **C** *Hurriedly* entering the kitchen.

16

LEVEL 5–6   WHAT DOES THE WRITER MEAN BUT NOT TELL YOU DIRECTLY?

3 Read the next scene, then explain how clues in a text help you to form opinions about characters.

> **TIP**
> ★ 'Explain' does not mean 'tell the story'. It means make points to answer the question using short quotations from the text.

Donna's bedroom. *She flops on the bed, and makes a call on her mobile to her friend Nadia. Switch to split screen so both Donna's and Nadia's faces are visible throughout the call.*

Nadia: Hi, Donna, how's things?
Donna: Same as usual. Mum's in a mood and she takes it out on me. I'd hardly got in the door before she started on at me.
Nadia: What about? The usual …?
Donna: No. Makes a change, doesn't it? I don't care if she doesn't like Neil. He's my boyfriend, not hers. No, this time she just blew her top when I said I wanted to have my dinner in front of the TV. She's so moody at the moment.
Nadia: Perhaps she's got something on her mind.
Donna: Yeh, making my life a misery.
Nadia: Well … I was thinking that she might be missing your dad.
Donna: What's that got to do with her making my life a misery? They never got on when they were together.
Nadia: What I mean is that she might be under pressure … you know, being a single mum now – money worries, that sort of thing. Missing him in that way.
Donna: If anyone is missing him, it's me. She didn't think about me when she told him to get out, did she?
Nadia: Hmm … well, look, Donna, do you want to come round here for a bite? Might take the pressure off both of you. I can help you out with that maths assignment. I know you've been putting off doing it. Come on, we'll get it done in no time.
Donna: What do you mean putting it off?
Nadia: Just trying to …
Donna: Well don't. I can look after myself, thanks very much.

Donna ends the call and Nadia's face fades from the screen.

4 What impression do you get of Nadia and Donna? Use examples from the script to support your answer.

LEVEL 5–6   READING SKILLS

Commenting on the organisation of a text (1)

> Level 5 readers can identify the pattern of ideas in a text and make comments about it.
> Level 6 readers can understand the reason why a writer places ideas in a particular order.

Look at this argument about school uniform. You will see that the writer uses a FOR + AGAINST + FOR organisation. Ending on a positive note is one way to persuade a reader that the writer is right.

School uniform is the same for everyone, which is fair.	However, it doesn't give pupils much freedom of expression.	Overall, it is usually a practical style that lets everyone focus on their work.
FOR	**AGAINST**	**FOR**

1 Read this web page from the charity Oxfam. Then highlight the topic sentences.

---

http://www.oxfam.org.uk/donate/yourmoney.html

How your money helps

You're only a few clicks away from providing the support that could change someone's life. It's amazing how much can be achieved with just a small amount of money from people like you and a little help from Oxfam.

Giving regularly really is the best way to support Oxfam. It means we have reliable income we can count on which allows us to plan in advance and budget more effectively.

What can you buy for 16p a day? You might think 'not much these days' but a gift of 16p a day (that's just £5 per month), can provide basic essentials like clean water and healthcare, and life-changing opportunities like education and small-business training to the people who need them most.

For every £1 you give to Oxfam

80p is spent directly on emergency, development and campaigning work

10p is spent on support and running costs

10p is invested to generate future income

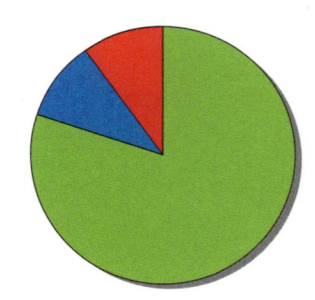

TIP ★ Topic sentences will help you to identify ideas.

LEVEL 5–6 — **COMMENTING ON THE ORGANISATION OF A TEXT**

At Level 6, readers are expected to identify the reason **why** a writer puts ideas in a particular order, e.g.:

> Level 5 part of answer
>
> **The writer begins the third paragraph with a question** to challenge the reader rather than just giving facts.
>
> Level 6 part of answer

2 How does the writer organise the text to have an impact on the reader?
Read these comments and mark them as Level 5 or Level 6. Then highlight the part of the response that makes it a Level 6 answer.

a) Paragraphs 1 and 4 are both about how little money is needed to make a difference.

b) Paragraph 3 gives general examples of how money can help. Paragraph 4 then gives precise information about how money is spent to show the reader that every penny counts.

c) The writer refers to money in paragraphs 3 and 4, and gives examples of how money is spent.

d) The first and last paragraphs are linked because they show readers that even a little makes a difference. The writer uses the first section to open up the idea and the last section to prove it.

3 In the bullet points, why has the writer presented the figures in this order?

_____

_____

_____

19

LEVEL 5–6

READING SKILLS

Commenting on the organisation of a text (2)

> **TIP** ★ Identify any link between the beginning and ending of a story. Then try to work out how the other sections fit together.

1 Read this text. It is the beginning of a story set in China about a young girl called Lu Si-yan.

> I loved my baby brother, until Uncle took me to market and sold me. He was the bright, shiny pebble in the water, the twinkling star in the sky. Until Uncle took me to market and sold me. Then I hated him.
>
> 'Lu Si-yan,' Uncle greeted me early one summer morning, 'today is a big day for you. From today, you must learn to find your own way in the muddy whirlpool of life. Your mother and I have given you a good start. Now it is your turn.'
>
> My mother stood in the shadows of our kitchen, but she didn't look at me and she didn't say a word. Uncle took me tightly by the wrist. As he led me from the house, my mother reached out her hand towards me and clawed the air as though trying to pull me back. Then she picked up my little brother and hid behind the door, but I saw her face wither with pain and, in that moment, fear gripped my heart.
>
> 'Where are you taking me, Uncle Ba?' I cried.
>
> *Spilled Water* by Sally Grindley

a) Underline the most shocking phrase in the first paragraph.
b) How does this link with the last sentence?
c) Why has the writer given away such important information in the first paragraph?

> **TIP** ★ A one-sentence summary of the 'job' of each section can help you to see a pattern in the text.

2 Use comments **A–D** to label paragraphs 2 and 3. Use the boxes beside the text.
  A The mother knows a terrible thing is about to happen.
  B The reader knows the girl is about to be tricked.
  C The writer shows the girl's emotions.
  D The uncle makes it sound like a good thing is going to happen

3 How does knowing that Lu Si-yan is going to be sold affect how you read the other paragraphs?

LEVEL 5–6 COMMENTING ON THE ORGANISATION OF A TEXT

TIP ★ Identify the 'job' of each section. Then consider why the writer put the sections in this order.

4 Read the opening of this novel about a boy in the 1800s who wants to be a sailor.

> One night at supper I told my father I wanted to become a sailor. He laughed at first, not taking me seriously. But when I insisted, his face grew darker.
>
> 'The Navy's a brutal calling, Sam, only suitable for brutal men. You're a thinker, you're a sensitive boy, and you're still young, for heaven's sake. I'll not have you waste your talents with the thugs and sweepings of our gaols that fill the Navy ships.' Then his voice softened. 'Besides – I want to see you grow up and marry. I want you to look after your mother and me in our old age! We don't want you getting yourself killed hundreds of miles away from home.'
>
> My mother stayed silent, but her eyes filled with tears. There had been four of us boys once, rather than two. Smallpox carried off my two younger brothers when I was six. Now there was just my older brother Thomas and me. He was more of a timid soul and not so interested in the world. It was Tom who would inherit my father's shop.
>
> My father had in mind that I would teach at the village school and help my uncle run his shop. A life selling groceries would suit Tom fine.
>
> But not me. I always wanted to escape from the vast, flat horizon of Norfolk, with only the flapping sails of a few creaking windmills to break the silence. Grey and grim it is for two-thirds of the year, with a biting wind coming straight off the North Sea. Reverend Chatham, our village parson, says there are barely three hundred people in the parish. Imagine just seeing those same few faces for the rest of your life?
>
> *Powder Monkey* by Paul Dowswell

What is the 'job' of each section? Write your answer alongside each paragraph.

5 How does the order of the information in the opening of this story help to keep the reader interested?

TIP ★ There may not be one correct answer to the practice question. You have to show that **you** can make connections and **explain** them to a teacher or examiner.

LEVEL 5–6   READING SKILLS

Commenting on how a writer uses language for effect (1)

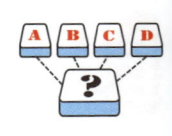

Level 5 readers can identify interesting language effects and make short comments about them.

Level 6 readers can give more detailed comments on a writer's use of language.

TIP
★ Read a text once to find out what happens.
Then read it again to identify interesting language.

1 This story was written in 1860. It is about an orphan boy, Pip. It begins with him crying at the family tombstone. But suddenly, he is not alone … Read it twice and make a note of any interesting language.

'Hold your noise!' cried a terrible voice, as a man started up from among the graves at the side of the church porch. 'Keep still, you little devil, or I'll cut your throat!'

A fearful man, all in coarse grey, with a great iron on his leg. A man with no hat, and with broken shoes, and with an old rag tied round his head. A man who had been soaked in water, and smothered in mud, and lamed by stones, and cut by flints, and stung by nettles, and torn by briars; who limped, and shivered, and glared and growled; and whose teeth chattered in his head as he seized me by the chin.

'O! Don't cut my throat, sir,' I pleaded in terror. 'Pray don't do it, sir.'

Great Expectations by Charles Dickens

a) Using different coloured highlighters, find examples in the text of:
   ★ repetition – a word or phrase repeated several times;
   ★ a list – it can be a list of words or phrases;
   ★ alliteration – words beginning with the same letter or sound.

b) How do these language effects help to make the man seem frightening?
   Sample Level 5 answer:
   'Glared and growled' help to make the man seem frightening and maybe a bit like an animal.

c) Circle the quotation in this answer. Underline the two short comments.

d) Now write an answer to explain the use of repetition and the list.

22

LEVEL 5–6   **COMMENTING ON HOW A WRITER USES LANGUAGE FOR EFFECT (1)**

> **TIP**
> ★ At Level 6, readers may pick the same quotations as at Level 5, but their comments are more detailed.

2 Read this text about a man, Victor Frankenstein, who creates a creature made from parts of other bodies. This is the moment the creature comes to life.

phrase to suggest dull light

It was on a <mark>dreary night of November</mark> that I beheld the accomplishment of my toils. With an anxiety that almost amounted to agony, I collected the instruments of life around me, that I might infuse a spark of being into the lifeless thing that lay at my feet. It was already one in the morning; the rain pattered dismally against the panes, and my candle was nearly burnt out, when, by the glimmer of the half-extinguished light, I saw the dull yellow eye of the creature open; it breathed hard, and a convulsive motion agitated its limbs.

Frankenstein by Mary Shelley

a) Sample text question:
How does the writer use language to create a miserable setting?
Highlight all the words or phrases linked to light or colour. Then build your answer like this:

> The writer makes the scene seem miserable by <mark>referring to dull light.</mark> It is <mark>'dreary'</mark>, <mark>which sounds dull and heavy</mark>, and <mark>darkness is suggested</mark> by <mark>'night'</mark> and <mark>'November'</mark>.

explanations linking quotations and question   *short quotations*

b) Choose two more words or phrases from the text to comment on in detail. Write a few sentences about the words as in the example above.

c) Underline three short explanations in your answer.

d) Now check your work. Do your comments:
   ★ link to the question?   **YES** or **NO**
   ★ use short supporting quotations?   **YES** or **NO**

23

LEVEL 5–6 READING SKILLS

Commenting on how a writer uses language for effect (2)

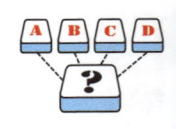

Writers sometimes use **contrast** to make an impression with language.

> **TIP** ★ A 'contrast' is like a 'difference'. When things are different from each other, you notice them more sharply.

1 Read this story, in which the writer presents the farmer as an unpleasant man right from the start.

> Mr Jones, of the Manor Farm, had locked the hen-houses for the night, but was too drunk to remember to shut the pop-holes. With the ring of light from his lantern **dancing from side to side,** he **lurched** across the yard, **kicked off** his boots at the back door, drew himself a last glass of beer from the barrel in the scullery, and made his way up to bed, where Mrs Jones was already snoring.
>
> As soon as the light in the bedroom went out there was a **stirring** and a **fluttering** all through the farm buildings. Word had gone round during the day that old Major, the prize Middle White boar, had had a strange dream on the previous night and wished to communicate it to the other animals. It had been agreed that they should all meet in the big barn as soon as Mr Jones was safely out of the way.
>
> *Animal Farm* by George Orwell

Complete this commentary on the language in the story by using the words in the box below to fill the gaps.

The words and phrases highlighted in **a)** _____ describe how Mr Jones moves. Those highlighted **b)** _____ describe the movements of other things. The fact that everything except Mr Jones moves in a **c)** _____ and **d)** _____ way makes him seem even **e)** _____ and **f)** _____.

| clumsier | yellow | interesting | slower | green | light |

24

LEVEL 5–6   COMMENTING ON HOW A WRITER USES LANGUAGE FOR EFFECT

2 Read this article, in which the writer 'plays' with language to make a serious article sound more fun.

How to invest in collectible toys

If you're clearing out the attic and just about to throw away your childhood toys, think again. They may be worth more than just sentimental value.

The magnetic pull of a toyshop is a standard childhood memory. And an early passion for Lego, Action Man or Barbie never quite fades. So it is not surprising that collectible toys are a prime investment, with select examples realising very grown-up prices at auction.

A white Steiff teddy bear from 1925, for example, fetched £25,200 – more than five times the estimate – at an auction house in 2006.

David Nathan of Vectis Toy Auctions says that older items – typically pre-1970s – are the safest bet, provided they are in mint condition and boxed. 'Some new toys will rocket in price; most won't. It is hard to make that call. With older items, you know whether or not there is a market. Even so, trends come and go. Antique dolls are weak at the moment, while teddies are strong, for example.'

He adds: 'One definite no-no should be all new limited-edition toys. Buyers almost always keep them in cabinets or whatever, so a perfect example is nothing rare. In contrast, 99 per cent of ordinary toys get play-worn, which means the boxed ones are special.'

> **TIP** ★ Word opposites can also build up a pattern for the writer to use, e.g. toys – serious stuff.

a) First, read the text. Then read again and highlight any words linked to toys or children that may be used to make the article sound more fun.

b) Explain how these words or phrases add humour to a serious business article.

> **TIP** ★ Remember: QUOTATION + EXPLANATION

25

LEVEL 5–6 **READING SKILLS**

Understanding the writer's viewpoint and the overall effect of the text (1)

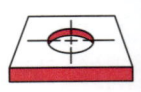

> **Level 5** readers can identify the purpose of a text and begin to explain the effect of the text on the reader.
>
> **Level 6** readers can explain how the writer achieves a purpose, using quotations and references from the text.

1 Read this autobiographical text by Roald Dahl. He recalls pretending to be ill, so he could be sent home from boarding school (which he hated). He is talking to the family doctor who is a friend of his mother's.

> He sat himself down behind his desk and fixed me with a penetrating but not unkindly eye. 'You're faking, aren't you?' he said.
>
> 'How do you know?' I blurted out.
>
> 'Because your stomach is soft and perfectly normal,' he answered. 'If you had had an inflammation down there, the stomach would have been hard and rigid. It's quite easy to tell.'
>
> I kept silent.
>
> 'I expect you're homesick,' he said.
>
> I nodded miserably.
>
> 'Everyone is at first,' he said. 'You have to stick it out. And don't blame your mother for sending you away to boarding school. She insisted you were too young to go, but it was I who persuaded her it was the right thing to do. Life is tough, and the sooner you learn how to cope with it the better for you.'
>
> 'What will you tell the school?' I asked him, trembling.
>
> 'I'll say you had a very severe infection of the stomach which I am curing with pills,' he answered smiling. 'It will mean that you must stay home for three more days. But promise me you won't try anything like this again …'
>
> *Boy* by Roald Dahl

a) On a separate piece of paper, try to answer the practice quesion below. You might find this type of question in your KS3 National Test.

PRACTICE QUESTION

What impressions are given about the young Roald Dahl as he sits in front of the doctor? Support you answer with references to the text.

(3 marks)

b) Now look at this pupil response. Is the answer correct or incorrect?

> **He's frightened because he has done something wrong and he thinks he might get into trouble.**

c) Look at the descriptions of Level 5 and Level 6 readers at the top of this page. What level do you think this answer is?

LEVEL 5–6 UNDERSTANDING THE WRITER'S VIEWPOINT ...

The answer was okay, but does not give the whole picture and there are no references or quotations to back it up.

> **TIP** ★ Take time to research a full answer.

2 Circle whether each of these statements is True or False.

   a) Roald Dahl owns up almost immediately.   True / False
   b) He's too frightened to make excuses.   True / False
   c) He becomes sad and fearful.   True / False
   d) He is amazed at the doctor's cleverness.   True / False
   e) He is disappointed that his plan did not work. True / False

   Now check the answer page.

3 Highlight in red the sentences that helped to build up your impression. They will give you the references or quotations you need to support your answer.

   If you've done this carefully, you have probably picked out these sentences.

   'How do you know?' I blurted out.

   I kept silent.

   I nodded miserably.

   'What will you tell the school?' I asked him, trembling.

> **TIP** ★ It is important to scan through the whole text to form an opinion rather than just look closely at one area. This will help you to do well in questions that give 3 or 5 marks.

4 Now write a better answer to the practice question on page 26. Use a separate piece of paper.

5 Use your research skills to answer this more difficult practice question:

PRACTICE QUESTION

What different impressions does the reader get about the doctor in this text? Support your answer with references from the text.

(3 marks)

LEVEL 5–6

READING SKILLS

Understanding the writer's viewpoint and the overall effect of the text (2)

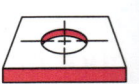

1. Read this text in which a school inspector has been asked to give advice on a particular pupil. Phinn describes what happened when he visited the school.

> When the children had taken off their coats and changed into their indoor shoes, they sat at their desks ready for the register to be called. All, that is, except one child. He was a sharp-faced boy of about nine or ten with a scattering of freckles, wavy red hair and a tight little mouth which curved downwards. This, I guessed, was Terry.
>
> *The Other Side of the Dale* by Gervase Phinn

2. The writer's purpose is to focus on one pupil. Complete this explanation of how the writer does this. Choose words from the words in the box to fill the gaps.

The writer sets the scene in the first sentence but then zooms in on one particular pupil in the sentence, 'All, that is, except one child.' That sentence is a) _____ and snappy so it focuses attention on that child. Next, the writer b) _____ that particular child in some detail. That makes the child more c) _____ for the reader. Then, the d) _____ sentence tells us the child's name. It sticks in the mind even more because it is the final e) _____ given in the paragraph.

| describes | short | last | impression | real |

TIP ★ A writer can have more than one purpose!

3. a) Is it a positive or negative impression of Terry?
   b) Highlight words and phrases in the story that support your opinion.
   c) Write a paragraph to explain how the writer creates this impression.

LEVEL 5–6 **UNDERSTANDING THE WRITER'S VIEWPOINT ...**

4 Read the next part of the story and see whether you were right.

> 'Come along, please, Terry,' said Miss Pilkington firmly, 'take your seat.'
>
> 'Who's he, then?' asked the child, pointing in my direction.
>
> 'That's Mr Phinn, and please don't point, it's rude.'
>
> 'Is he a copper?'
>
> 'Just take a seat will you, please, Terry,' said the teacher.
>
> 'He looks like a copper. Are you a copper?'
>
> 'Terry, will you take a seat,' repeated the teacher firmly.
>
> 'I can smell coppers a mile off.' The child slumped into a chair. 'He's either a copper or a probation officer.'
>
> 'And take what you are chewing out of your mouth, please, Terry,' said Miss Pilkington.
>
> 'Haven't finished it yet.' He looked back at me. 'I bet he is a copper.'
>
> 'Put what you are chewing in here, please Terry,' said the teacher firmly, holding up a waste-paper basket.
>
> The boy ambled to the front and dropped a bullet of chewing gum in the bin.
>
> *The Other Side of the Dale* by Gervase Phinn

Two people are now in focus: Miss Pilkington and Terry.
Try this practice question about these characters.

PRACTICE QUESTION

What impressions are you given of Terry and Miss Pilkington? You should consider:
★ what Terry says;
★ what he does;
★ how Miss Pilkington talks.

Support your answer with brief quotations from the text.

(3 marks)

_____
_____
_____
_____
_____
_____

TIP ★ Use your highlighter to mark out useful quotations.

Test yourself: practice reading tests

Reading test 1: Story Maker

Text A

This text is from a story set in Afghanistan in 1975. Amir is the son of a wealthy man. Hassan is a servant in the house but Amir treats him as a friend. Amir can read fluently but Hassan has received no education and cannot.

One day, in July 1973, I played another little trick on Hassan. I was reading to him, and suddenly I strayed from the written story. I pretended I was reading from the book, flipping pages regularly, but I had abandoned the text altogether, taken over the story, and made up my own. Hassan, of course, was oblivious to this. To him, the words on the page were a scramble of codes, indecipherable, mysterious. Words were secret doorways and I held all the keys. After, I started to ask him if he'd liked the story, a giggle rising in my throat, when Hassan began to clap.

'What are you doing?' I said.

'That was the best story you've read me in a long time,' he said, still clapping.

I laughed. 'Really?'

'Really.'

'That's fascinating,' I muttered. I meant it too. This was … wholly unexpected. 'Are you sure, Hassan?'

He was still clapping. 'It was great, Amir. Will you read me more of it tomorrow?'

'Fascinating,' I repeated, a little breathless, feeling like a man who discovers buried treasure in his own backyard. Walking down the hill, thoughts were exploding in my head like fireworks. Best story you've read me in a long time, he'd said. I had read him a lot of stories.

The Kite Runner by Khaled Hosseini

LEVEL 5–6 **TEST YOURSELF: PRACTICE READING TESTS**

1 Answer True or False to these statements.

   a) Hassan thought Amir was reading a story.   True ☐ False ☐

   b) Amir was at first amused by the way he had tricked Hassan.   True ☐ False ☐

   c) Hassan was laughing at Amir.   True ☐ False ☐

   d) Amir knew Hassan would prefer his made-up story.   True ☐ False ☐

AF2 — 1 mark

2 *Words were secret doorways and I held all the keys.*
Explain what this sentence tells you about the relationship between Hassan and Amir?

_____
_____
_____

AF3 — 1 mark

3 What is the effect of the ellipsis (…) in: *This was … wholly unexpected?*

_____
_____

AF5 — 1 mark

4 *exploding in my head like fireworks*
What is the effect of using these words to describe Amir's thoughts?

_____
_____
_____

AF5 — 2 marks

5 Explain how the writer shows Amir's mood changing through the text. Use quotations to support your opinions.

_____
_____
_____
_____
_____
_____
_____
_____

AF6 — 3 marks

Text B

Read this account by Dick King-Smith, who is the author of the children's story *The Sheep-Pig*. The story was made into a successful film called *Babe*. Here, he describes how he and his wife, Myrtle, felt when they watched it.

The opening credits came up on the huge screen. Among them: ADAPTED FROM THE BOOK BY DICK-KING SMITH.

We nudged each other.

Myrtle and I sat enthralled throughout the film. It was soon plain to us that the adaptation from the book had been wonderfully well done.

There were differences, of course – there always are when you change something from one medium to another. There were additional pieces of action, and quite an array of new characters – another dog, the cat, that marvellous duck – but the director had stuck pretty faithfully to the central theme of my original story: the tale of an orphaned piglet who is adopted by a farmer and his sheep-dog. This little pig, by virtue of his intelligence and determination, his courage, and especially through his realisation that politeness pays, comes eventually to win the Grand Challenge Sheep-dog Trials. One particular thing about the film that delighted me was that, as soon as I set eyes on the actor who played Farmer Hogget, I saw to my amazement that he was the spitting image of the imaginary figure I'd had in my head when I wrote the book all those years before.

I've seen Babe six times now and every time I've laughed and I've cried, but of course at that first viewing we had no idea that the film would become such a huge international success. During the many years that it was in the making, I'd written masses of other children's books. But *The Sheep-Pig* was to be the one that would bring me so much publicity and do me such a lot of good.

If you were to ask me to choose a favourite from among the dozens and dozens of books I've produced, I would probably say I think it may be the best.

It's always nice for me to think that, in a funny way, Babe was born here, in the little village where we live. I mean that he was born in my head, in my imagination, thanks to our annual village Summer Fete.

One particular year I was in charge of the Guess-the-Weight-of-the Pig stall, and I must, I suppose, have thought as I stood upon the village green, recording people's guesses and taking their money, that it was such a shame that such a lovely little pink pig should end up, once he was big enough, in the deep-freeze.

Suppose fate had something quite different in store for him? Suppose he should go and live on a farm, with a sheep-dog as his foster-mother? Suppose he should want to do what she did?

He couldn't be a sheep-dog.

But he could be a sheep-pig.

Chewing the Cud by Dick King-Smith

LEVEL 5–6
TEST YOURSELF: PRACTICE READING TESTS

6 Answer True or False to these statements.

   a) Farmer Hogget was based on a real character.   True ☐   False ☐

   b) As soon as Dick King-Smith saw the film,
       he knew it would be a world-wide success.   True ☐   False ☐

   c) The film made Dick King-Smith better known.   True ☐   False ☐

   d) The film was made very quickly.   True ☐   False ☐

AF2 — 1 mark

7 Tick the statement that best describes Dick King-Smith's reaction to the changes made when the book was turned into a film.

★ He was surprised and pleased about the changes. ☐

★ He thought the film director had made too many changes. ☐

★ He expected some changes and was pleased with them. ☐

★ He thought the additional characters spoilt the theme of the original story. ☐

AF3 — 1 mark

8 Refer to the paragraph beginning *I've seen Babe six times now* … to the end of the text. How does the writer feel about the pig character, Babe, that he created?

Support your answer with brief quotations from the text.

_____
_____
_____
_____
_____
_____
_____

AF6 — 3 marks

9 On a separate piece of paper, explain how the writer builds up a sense of increasing excitement in the final part of the text, from *It's always nice for me to think* … to *be a sheep-pig*. You should comment on:

★   his description of how the idea for his story started;

★   the effect of his use of questions;

★   the effect of the two single-line paragraphs at the end.

Support your answer with references to the text.

AF4 — 5 marks

LEVEL 5–6 — READING SKILLS

Reading test 2: Attack!

Text A

Read this account of gladiators in combat. In Ancient Rome, gladiators fought to the death in front of huge audiences. In this account, one gladiator is armed with a sword and buckler (a small, round shield). The other is named 'Fisher' because he uses a weighted net and a trident (a three-pronged spear).

The roar which greeted the pair of fighters had fallen to a breathless hush. In the centre of the arena the two men were being placed by the captain of gladiators; placed with exquisite care, ten paces apart, with no advantage of light or wind allowed to either. The thing was quickly and competently done, and the captain stepped back to the barriers. For what seemed a long time neither of the two moved. Moment followed moment, and still they remained motionless, the centre of all that great circle of staring faces. Then, very slowly, the swordsman began to move. Never taking his eyes from his adversary, he slipped one foot in front of the other; crouching a little, covering his body with the round buckler, inch by inch he crept forward, every muscle tensed to spring when the time came.

The Fisher stood still as ever, poised on the balls of his feet, the trident in his left hand, his right lost in the folds of the net. Just beyond reach of the net, the swordsman checked for a long, agonising moment, and then sprang in. His attack was so swift that the flung net flew harmlessly over his head, and the Fisher leapt back and sideways to avoid his thrust, then whirled about and ran for his life, gathering his net for another cast as he ran, with the young swordsman hard behind him …

… The two came flying round the curve of the barrier, and the Fisher whirled about and flung once more. The net whipped out like a dark flame; it licked round the running swordsman, so intent on his chase that he had forgotten to guard for it; the weights carried the deadly folds across and across again, and a howl burst from the crowd as he crashed headlong and rolled over, helplessly meshed as a fly in a spider's web.

The Eagle of the Ninth by Rosemary Sutcliffe

LEVEL 5–6   TEST YOURSELF: PRACTICE READING TESTS

1 Put the events in the order they happened.
One has been done as an example.

1	_E_	**A** The Fisher was chased by the swordsman.
2	___	**B** Both gladiators faced each other, motionless.
3	___	**C** The swordsman made the first move.
4	___	**D** The net was thrown but missed its target.
5	___	**E** The captain moved aside after setting the gladiators in place.
6	___	**F** With his second throw, the Fisher trapped his victim.

AF2 [ ] 1
2 marks

2 What three things did the captain have to check before the contest could begin?

_____
_____
_____

AF2 [ ] 2
1 mark

3 What does *breathless hush* in the first sentence suggest about the mood of the crowd?

_____
_____
_____

AF3 [ ] 3
1 mark

4 From paragraph 3, what do these words suggest about the net and its movements?

The net whipped out like a dark flame; it licked round the running swordsman.

like a dark flame: _____

licked: _____

AF5 [ ] 4
2 marks

5 Explain how the writer uses the order of events in paragraph 1 to build a sense of expectation for the reader. Refer closely to the text to support your answer.

_____
_____
_____
_____
_____

AF4 [ ] 5
3 marks

| LEVEL 5–6 | READING SKILLS |

Text B

Read this text about Rodney Fox. On 8 December 1963, he was competing in the South Australia Spearfishing Championships. This involves swimming in the water with a spear to catch fish. He had won the title the previous year, but this time things were going to be different.

Fox was in superb form, drifting, gliding, spearing his quick elusive targets with the practised ease of a born competitor. With an hour left, he looked likely to win the title again. He was one kilometre (1110 yards) offshore, drifting in for a shot at a dusky morwong*, sure of the kill, his finger tensing on the trigger, when something huge hit his left side – 'it was like being hit by a train' – knocking the gun from his hand and tearing the mask from his face. His next impression was of speed, surging through the water faster than he had ever done, a gurgling roar in his ears, and of the easy, rhythmical power of the shark, holding him as a dog does a bone.

With his right arm he clawed for the shark's eyes; it released its grip and Fox instinctively thrust out his right arm to ward it off. The arm disappeared into the shark's mouth, lacerating** the underside on the bottom row of teeth. As the horrified Fox jerked it out, the arm caught the upper jaw. In extremity men do amazing things: Fox, terrified of the open maw***, tried to bear-hug the shark, to wrap his arms and legs round the abrasive skin, to get a purchase**** away from the teeth. It did not work – the shark was too big for him to hug.

He suddenly realised another need even more urgent than fending off the shark – air. He pushed away, kicked for the surface, gulped one breath and looked down on a scene that burnt itself into his memory. His mask gone, his vision blurred, he floated in a pink sea, and a few metres away was a pointed nose, and a mouth lined with razor sharp teeth, coming at him.

*dusky morwong – a type of fish
**lacerating – tearing
***maw – mouth
****get a purchase – get a hold

LEVEL 5–6   TEST YOURSELF: PRACTICE READING TESTS

6 The writer deliberately uses contrast in paragraph 1. Complete this table to explain how the mood of the first half of the paragraph is contrasted to the second half.

Mood in first half of paragraph	Mood in second half of paragraph

AF4

6

2 marks

7 In paragraph 3, why did Fox swim to the surface?

_____
_____

AF2

7

1 mark

8 *a scene that burnt itself into his memory*
Give two reasons why *burnt* is an effective word to use here.

_____
_____

AF5

8

2 marks

9 How does the writer use language to create horror in paragraph 2? You should comment on the writer's choice of:
  ★ particular words;
  ★ sentence structures;
  ★ punctuation.

Use brief quotations to support your answer.

_____
_____
_____
_____
_____
_____
_____
_____
_____

AF5

9

5 marks

37

LEVEL 5–6

Introduction to writing skills

Writing is marked in three separate ways in the National Tests:

★ sentence structure and punctuation;
★ text structure and organisation;
★ using an appropriate style for the task and the reader.

The following sections of this book will help you to revise and practise one skill at a time. This approach helps you to focus closely on each element of writing so that you can achieve a Level 6 standard when you combine all the skills together.

Sentence structure and punctuation

In this section of the book, you will revise and practise using the following.

★ **Connectives** (pages 40–41):

Level 5 writers use a variety of connectives and sometimes use them to begin a sentence.
Level 6 writers select appropriate connectives to help the reader make links between ideas.

★ **Adjectives** (pages 42–43):

Level 5 writers add detail with interesting adjectives and longer phrases and clauses.
Level 6 writers add detail with well-selected words and phrases.

★ **Adverbs** (pages 44–45):

Level 5 writers use a wider range of adverbs and some adverbial phrases.
Level 6 writers can use adverbial phrases to add detail.

★ **Punctuation** (pages 46–47):

Level 5 writers use a wider range of punctuation accurately.
Level 6 writers use a full range of punctuation accurately.

Text structure and organisation

In this section of the book, you will revise and practise using the following.

★ **Paragraph and text organisation devices** (pages 48–49):

Level 5 writers give openings and closings to their work.
Level 6 writers give clear openings and closings, and make links between sections.

WRITING SKILLS

Using an appropriate style for the task and the reader

In the National Tests, each writing task is linked to a particular form of writing – for example, persuasive, descriptive or narrative writing. This book cannot teach you everything you need to know about a particular form of writing, but it will give you practice with helpful techniques to improve your writing in a range of different styles.

★ **Improving your informative writing** (pages 50–51):

Level 5 writers choose language to inform and interest the reader.

Level 6 writers use language confidently to convince the reader.

★ **Improving your persuasive writing** (pages 52–53):

Level 5 writers use some techniques to influence a reader.

Level 6 writers can produce persuasive writing using a variety of techniques.

★ **Improving your imaginative writing** (pages 54–55):

Level 5 writers tell a story, making careful decisions about character and action.

Level 6 writers build atmosphere and character in stories with careful choice of words.

★ **Improving your writing to review** (pages 56–57):

Level 5 writers explain opinions clearly and politely.

Level 6 writers explain opinions in detail, using an appropriate tone.

Combining all your skills

After practising all your skills separately, put them together to do a National Test-style Writing Test (page 59). The practice test includes a longer and a shorter writing test. Mark the writing test yourself using the self-assessment grid on page 61.

Each skill is a brick in the wall to help your writing become well-constructed and strong.

- Connectives
- adjectives and adverbs
- punctuation
- paragraph organisation
- topic sentences
- links between paragraphs
- relevant and developed ideas
- clear signals to the reader
- vocabulary to suit the topic

LEVEL 5–6   WRITING SKILLS

Using a wider range of connectives

Level 5 writers use a variety of connectives and sometimes use them to begin a sentence.
Level 6 writers select appropriate connectives to help the reader make links between ideas.

1 Revise the connectives you know how to use.
Imagine you are a young writer working on the opening of a story:
Agent Swift – Special Operations Squad.
Here are some ideas.

> Agent Swift was looking at his watch. He heard the shot. He jumped up. He grabbed his gun from the table. He quickly checked the gun was loaded. He ran to the window to look down at the street. The street looked no different. He thought there was something odd about it.

You want to build up the sentences to give more variety. Fill in the gaps with your choice of words.

- unless
- where
- as

- where
- when
- wherever

Agent Swift was looking at his watch **a)** _____ he heard the the shot. He grabbed his gun from the table **b)** _____ he jumped up. He quickly checked the gun was loaded **c)** _____ he ran to the window to look down at the street. The street looked no different **d)** _____ he thought there was something odd about it.

- before
- although
- after

- although
- before
- until

40

LEVEL 5–6 — SENTENCE STRUCTURE AND PUNCTUATION

Although different connectives have been used, they could be better placed to achieve a more interesting effect.

2 Which connectives would you use to open these sentences?

> Agent Swift was looking at his watch when he heard the shot.
> a) _____ he grabbed his gun from the table, he jumped up.
> He quickly checked the gun was loaded before he ran to the window to look down at the street. b) _____ the street looked no different, he thought there was something odd about it.

TIP ★ When you begin a sentence with a connective, use a comma at the end of the first part. If you read the sentence aloud, you can hear a slight pause there.

3 Look at the next part of the story. Practise putting the connectives and commas in the right places.

> It was then Agent Swift realised that the trees had no leaves. They were completely bare. a) _____ he had walked down that same street two hours ago every tree was full of fluttering leaves. He looked at the calendar on the office wall to check the date – 10th July. b) _____ he knew it was mid-summer it looked like mid-winter outside!

When   Even though

TIP ★ Choosing the right place for the connective is important. If the connective is placed first, attention is focused onto that part of the sentence.

4 Write the next paragraph of the story, trying to include these connectives:

as soon as   before   while   whereas   whoever

TIP ★ Vary the position of the connective, depending on which piece of information you want to draw attention to.

LEVEL 5–6 **WRITING SKILLS**

Adding detail with adjectives

> Level 5 writers add detail with interesting adjectives and longer phrases and clauses.
> **Level 6 writers add detail with well-selected words and phrases.**

Carefully chosen adjectives, or pairs of adjectives, help to create deliberate effects in your writing.

1 Read this extract from a story. Ignore the numbers for the moment.

> Even though the room was empty, I could still sense her (1) presence.
> I recalled the look on her (2) face as she turned to face me. I would never forget the sound of her (3) voice as she passed close by on her way out.
> That (4) smile of hers would stay with me to the end of my days.

2 Put one adjective by each of the numbers to turn the extract into the start of a romance or a horror story.

ROMANCE
1 _____
2 _____
3 _____
4 _____

HORROR
1 _____
2 _____
3 _____
4 _____

Sometimes more than one adjective can be used to intensify the effect you want to create. These can be joined by 'and' or by a comma, e.g.:

As I left the cold **and** empty house, I knew I would never return.

As I left the cold**,** empty house, I knew I would never return.

Doing that too often would be repetitive. It's something to be done selectively.

3 Add another adjective to the ones you have chosen for numbers (1) and (4). Decide whether you want to add a comma or use 'and'. Do what you think creates the best effect.

4 Consider how you can use alliteration to create an even more noticeable effect. Instead of 'cold and empty', the adjective combination could be:

As I left the **c**old and **c**avernous house ...

As I left the **e**erie, **e**vil-smelling house ...

LEVEL 5–6   **SENTENCE STRUCTURE AND PUNCTUATION**

5 This mystery story needs more detail. Put one single adjective or a set of double adjectives in each sentence. The boxed list is more than you need. There isn't a correct answer; it's up to you to create the effect you want.

Now copy out **your** version of how the story should start.

> As soon as I had unpacked my case, I could hear voices in the next room. The language intrigued me. The sounds were unlike anything I had heard before. Then the music started. It was the music that awakened a memory in me.

> strange, harsh
> unearthly
> sweet, soft
> loud
> beautiful
> weird
> dark and depressing
> unpleasant

6 Compare your new version with this one. Yours may be much more interesting!

> As soon as I had unpacked my case, I could hear beautiful voices in the next room. The sweet, soft language intrigued me.
> The unearthly sounds were unlike anything I had heard before. Then the weird music started. It was the music which awakened a dark and depressing memory in me.

TIP ★ Remember: adding lots of adjectives doesn't always improve your writing. They have to be well-chosen.

7 Show how well you can use adjectives (and other words!) in your own writing. Pick one topic from below. Then write the first paragraph using about 100 words. Remember to use:

★ single adjectives;
★ one pair of adjectives;
★ one pair of alliterated adjectives.

Topics
★ A war story
★ A science-fiction story
★ A film review
★ A description of a sporting event
★ A report about a school trip

LEVEL 5–6 **WRITING SKILLS**

Adding detail with adverbial phrases

> **Level 5** writers use a wider range of adverbs and some adverbial phrases.
> **Level 6** writers can use adverbial phrases to add detail.

This story is about a boy who has run away from home. In this section, he is caught stealing a packet of sandwiches from a shop.

> When Ivan rushed into the shop, he saw the reason for all the shouting. His wife was struggling with a young boy who was fighting to get out of the door. Ivan didn't pause to think and he ran over, grabbed the boy's arm and twisted it behind his back.

This story needs more pace and drama. Re-draft to…

> Ivan *immediately* saw the reason for all the shouting. His wife was struggling with a young boy who was *savagely* fighting to get out of the door. Ivan ran over and *swiftly* grabbed the boy's arm and twisted it behind his back.

This writing would achieve Level 5.

1 Read the next paragraph of the story. Put the adverbs beside it into different places in the sentences, e.g. before the verb, after the verb, to start the sentence.

> His wife explained what had happened. The boy had grabbed a packet of sandwiches, stuffed them under his jacket and tried to run off without paying. Ivan realised the boy was crying and let go of his arm but he stood in the doorway to stop any escape.

breathlessly
suddenly
firmly
quietly

TIP ★ Practising with lots of adverbs is a good exercise but using too many adverbs is not good for your style.

LEVEL 5–6   **SENTENCE STRUCTURE AND PUNCTUATION**

Detail can be added with 'adverbial phrases'. These are groups of words that describe the verb, e.g.:

[verb]   [adverbial phrase]

The young boy was fighting with all his might to get out of the door.

2 Adverbial phrases can be added to the verb using 'with'. Add the phrases in the box to the story.

'You realise I'm going to have to call the police about this?' The boy stopped crying a) _____ but didn't say anything. 'Maria, get on the phone, will you?' His wife went behind the counter, got out her mobile and keyed in the emergency call. Ivan looked closely at the boy and realised b) _____ he knew him. 'Hang on a minute, Maria. I think I know this lad.'

He'd seen the boy before, but where? His local church … that was it! He'd seen this lad singing in the church choir, yet here he was shoplifting. He squatted down and looked the boy in the eyes, and he said, 'What's all this about, then?' The boy looked back at him c) _____ .

     with a quick wipe of his eyes   with a defiant glare   with surprise

TIP ★ Use these phrases with care.
The best thing for your writing is variety.

3 Use these writer's notes to complete the final paragraph of this story. Write about ten sentences. Include adverbs and adverbial phrases.

Grabs mobile off Ivan's wife
Stamps on it
Pushes over one of the display stands
Dodges round Ivan
Out into the street
Too quick for Ivan to catch
Ivan stands panting at street corner
Watches helplessly as boy disappears in the park across the main road

45

LEVEL 5–6 WRITING SKILLS

Using a full range of punctuation

Level 5 writers use a wider range of punctuation accurately.
Level 6 writers use a full range of punctuation accurately.

1 Tick all the punctuation items you are confident with. Practise those you are not so happy about.

Checklist

Full stops: ☐ I'm sure I don't need to explain these.

Commas for clauses: ☐ Although you are good at punctuation, a little revision always helps.

Commas as brackets: ☐ A lot of people, myself included, make some slips of punctuation.

Full punctuation of speech: ☐ My old teacher used to say, 'Punctuation keeps the train of your ideas on track.'

Semi-colons: ☐ It's great to remember my old school; I had a wonderful time there.

2 Punctuate this paragraph using the following punctuation:
   ★ commas;
   ★ full stops;
   ★ a question mark;
   ★ speech marks;
   ★ one semi-colon.

> The interview had been arranged for 10 o'clock and I arrived at reception 10 minutes early I wanted to make a good impression my father who had been in the army for 20 years had drummed into me the importance of being on time On time means you're on the ball he used to say to me it was a lesson I had never forgotten it served me well that day if I hadn't have been early I wouldn't have seen the man who staggered out of the lift he was holding a blood-stained handkerchief to his face and looked as if he was about to faint a strange thought crossed my mind was he on the interview list before me I offered to help him but he left the building muttering no job's worth that when I looked at my watch I saw my turn had come.

46

LEVEL 5–6   SENTENCE STRUCTURE AND PUNCTUATION

Revising semi-colons

Use a semi-colon (;) when you want to show a connection between two sentences, e.g. when the second sentence depends on what is described in the first sentence.

> It was a beautiful day. I decided to go and explore what the resort had to offer.

→

> It was a beautiful day; I decided to go and explore what the resort had to offer.

If you want to show the reader you decided to explore the resort because it was a beautiful day, use a semi-colon.

TIP ★ Use semi-colons carefully. They lose their effect if you use too many.

3 Highlight two sentences in each example that you think could be joined by a semi-colon.

A
It was Saturday so I woke later than usual. My mum was clattering around the kitchen and Dad was out playing golf. My sister had gone shopping. Saturday belonged to me. I could do just what I wanted. Well, that's what I thought.

B
The car ate up the miles of empty road. John looked around at the strange landscape and he thought back to how this journey had all started. It all began one year ago. In those 12 months he had changed so much. His thoughts were interrupted by the wail of a police siren.

4 a) Punctuate the paragraph below, then write out your version. Use these guidelines:
- ★ change most commas to full stops;
- ★ change one comma to a semi-colon;
- ★ keep one comma.

> The waiting crowd suddenly lost patience, I was caught up in the rush of people and carried along, bounced this way and that, I was like a cork in a rushing stream, suddenly a shot rang out and the crowd stumbled to a stop, a soldier was on the bridge and he was holding a rifle, it was pointed straight at the crowd, some sort of control had at last been established.

There is more than one answer, but you are now at a level where you can choose the effect you want.

b) Now write out a differently punctuated version. What is the difference you have created?

LEVEL 5–6   WRITING SKILLS

Improve the organisation of your writing

Level 5 writers give openings and closings to their work.
Level 6 writers give clear openings and closings, and make links between sections.

Readers need signposts to help them through a piece of writing. This helps them to understand and agree with, or get involved in, your writing.

1 Words that work as signposts are helpful to a writer and reader.
Add these words to the table below:

- ★ finally
- ★ next
- ★ first
- ★ however
- ★ eventually
- ★ despite this
- ★ in contrast
- ★ soon
- ★ afterwards
- ★ meanwhile
- ★ in addition
- ★ after this

Words that give order to instructions	Words that show time in a story	Words that link ideas in an argument

48

LEVEL 5–6　　　　　　　　　　　　　　　　　　　　　TEXT STRUCTURE AND ORGANISATION

Linking words and phrases prepare readers for the direction you will take them in.
Practise using linking sections in the tasks below.

2 Continue this story in two different ways using the handwritten words to begin the next paragraph.

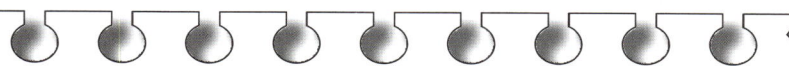

> I hated my name, hated my curly hair, and especially hated the shape of my ears.

In contrast, …　　Eventually, …

_____
_____
_____
_____

3 Continue this news article in three different ways using the linking words below.

> The fairy tale goes like this: they are high-school sweethearts from a small town. He graduates from high school, becomes a soldier and goes to war.

Despite this, …　　　　However, …　　　　As soon as …

_____
_____
_____
_____

> **TIP** ★ Not all links have to be made using these words. Sometimes the content of the sections makes a clear link.

49

LEVEL 5–6　　　　　　　　　　　　　　　　　　　　　　　　　　　　WRITING SKILLS

Improve your informative writing

> Level 5 writers choose language to inform and interest the reader.
> **Level 6 writers use language confidently to convince the reader.**

1 Imagine your headteacher has decided to change the existing school uniform and replace it with a more traditional style of blazer, with smart trousers for the boys and straight skirts for the girls. Read this item in your school newsletter, which the head has written to explain the decision.

New Street High School

After careful thought and close consultation with parents, I have decided to make a change to the existing school uniform.

I, and many others, felt that the existing uniform was in need of a radical overhaul. The blue sweatshirt and grey trousers did not seem to fit in with the new image of the school that we all wish to promote. Too often, the sweatshirt became a grubby, sloppy-looking item of clothing. Many pupils have suggested that they felt the sweatshirt was too informal and better suited to the gym rather than the classroom. The trousers were not popular with many of the girls.

The new uniform will create a more mature and business-like atmosphere. It has been designed by a leading fashion expert and is intended to suggest the type of clothes worn by successful men and women of the world of work. Several pupils have tried on the designs and assured me that they felt both comfortable and smart in them.

I will be sending to all parents/guardians a leaflet that contains photographs of the new uniform, as well as a list of prices and suppliers. This should be with you by the end of term.

I know you will support the school in this new, and exciting, venture.

Annotations:
- Introduces subject matter in a formal tone.
- Also claims he has a lot of support.
- Topic is old uniform. Adds detail to explanation to make a more convincing case.
- Moves to new topic – the new uniform. Piles up positive vocabulary to promote the idea.
- Moves to topic of what is going to happen next.
- Strong conclusion.

LEVEL 5–6   USING AN APPROPRIATE STYLE

You might, or might not, agree with the views of the head, but the explanation is clear and strong.

2 Find examples of these features in the head's explanation and highlight them in the text.

   ★ Clear introduction.
   ★ Clear paragraph structure with topic sentences.
   ★ Careful use of details and vocabulary to support point of view.
   ★ Adopts a formal tone to suggest authority.
   ★ Strong conclusion.

3 Choose **one** of the following topics and explain your views in an article for the school newsletter. Write your explanation following the model of the teacher on page 50.

> **Topics**
>   ★ Remove all soft-drinks vending machines from a school site.
>   ★ Boys and girls should be educated in separate schools.
>   ★ Pupils should be able to leave school at 15 years of age.

51

LEVEL 5–6 WRITING SKILLS

Improve your persuasive writing

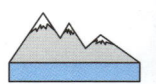

> Level 5 writers use some techniques to influence a reader.
> **Level 6 writers can produce pursuasive writing using a variety of techniques.**

Persuasive techniques help to get your audience's attention and convince them of your ideas.

1. Read this speech by Martin Luther King, a civil rights activist campaigning for racial equality in the USA in the 1960s.

   There are many techniques here that Level 6 writers can adopt.

   > *I have a dream* that one day this nation will rise up and live out the true meaning of its creed: 'We hold these truths to be self-evident, that all men are created equal.'
   >
   > *I have a dream* that one day on the red hills of Georgia, the sons of former slaves and the sons of former slave owners will be able to sit down together at the table of brotherhood.
   >
   > I have a dream that one day even the state of Mississippi, a state sweltering with the heat of injustice, sweltering with the heat of oppression, will be transformed into an oasis of freedom and justice.
   >
   > I have a dream that my four little children will one day live in a nation where they will not be judged by the colour of their skin but by the content of their character.
   >
   > I have a *dream* today!

   a) Label the highlighted text with the techniques in the left-hand column.

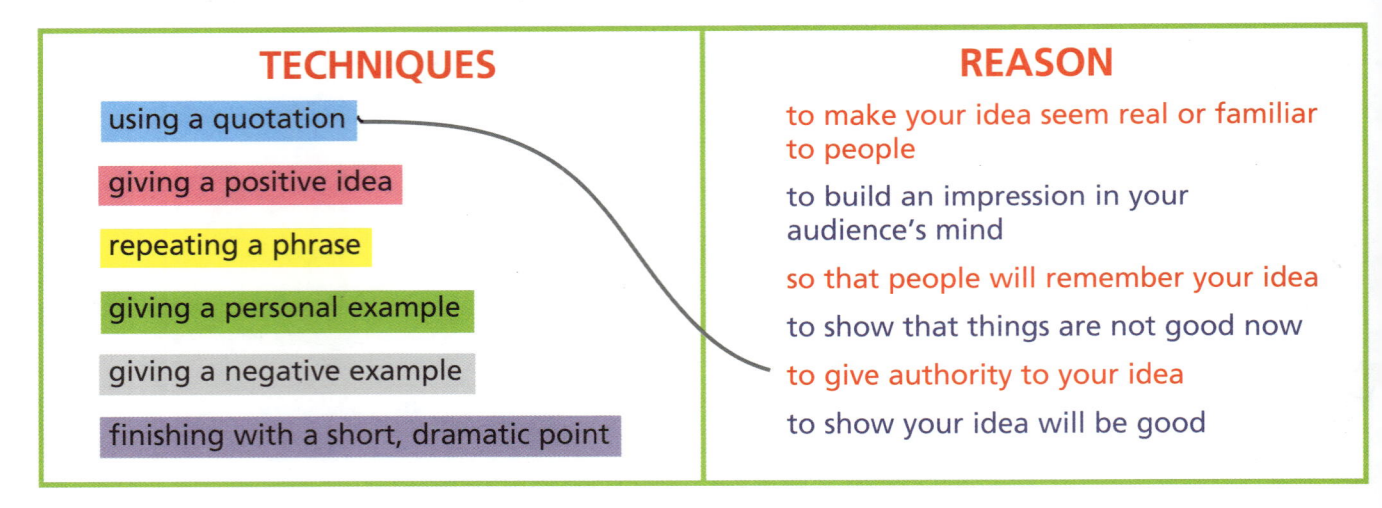

TECHNIQUES	REASON
using a quotation	to make your idea seem real or familiar to people
giving a positive idea	to build an impression in your audience's mind
repeating a phrase	so that people will remember your idea
giving a personal example	to show that things are not good now
giving a negative example	to give authority to your idea
finishing with a short, dramatic point	to show your idea will be good

   b) Match the techniques with the reason why they have been used. One has been done for you.

2. Make a list, in your own words, of techniques to use in a persuasive speech.

LEVEL 5-6 IMPROVE YOUR WRITING STYLE

Emotive language

Language that appeals to the emotions of your reader works well in persuasive writing. It is known as **emotive language**.

3 Imagine pupils at your school have voted to get rid of school uniform. Your job is to convince parents and teachers it's a good idea.

  a) Read this speech from someone who wants to keep school uniform.
  Identify the persuasive techniques that have been used by using the boxes and drawing lines to examples in the text. Use your own list and the techniques on page 52.

  > Uniform offers a sense of identity. The army, the police and the health service all use uniforms to give their members the sense that they belong to an organisation. School uniform is like this too; it gives everyone an equal opportunity to show they are a part of the community of the school. It also presents an identifiable sign to the general public that we are proud to belong to the school.

  > Uniform offers equality. After the initial expense of buying a uniform, parents do not have to worry about buying the latest brand name clothes so that their children will 'fit in'. Uniform is what it says: the same for everyone.

  > Uniform makes life easy. It removes the need to make difficult decisions about 'what to wear' each morning. I know, from experience, that having to think about breakfast is enough in the mornings – let alone what colour socks to wear!

  > Basically, uniform works for schools. Don't undo the good work.

  b) Prepare a speech to persuade parents and teachers that non-uniform is the right way to go. Use as many persuasive techniques as you can.

  c) Check your work to identify the techniques you have used.

  d) Think about a redraft. How would you improve the speech?

53

LEVEL 5–6 WRITING SKILLS

Improve your imaginative writing

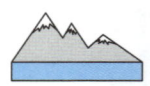

Level 5 writers tell a story, making careful decisions about character and action.
Level 6 writers build atmosphere and character in stories with careful choice of words.

1 Read texts **A** and **B**, which both respond to the task: *Write a story about discovering an object that reminds you of your past*. The pieces are roughly the same length, but they achieve different effects.

A

The further I went up, the darker it was getting. Soon the darkness of the room was dazzling and there was only the light of my mobile phone to keep me from not getting lost or tripping over an object and injuring myself.

There it was – the attic door. I cautiously opened the door. I was almost frightened. I hadn't been up there for years. Every visible object was smothered in a thick coat of dust and fly-infested cobwebs.

B

I asked mum where it was and she said that it might still be in the loft. I asked her if I could go up and have a look and she said I could so I got the ladder, which was getting old. The steps creaked and it looked very wobbly. I lifted the loft lid and stepped inside. The blackness was blinding. I felt around trying to find the light cord. Yes, I found it, pulled it and a very dull bulb came on.

2 One of the texts above is Level 5 and one is Level 6.
   a) Which do you think is Level 6?
   b) How do you know?

54

LEVEL 5–6   **USING AN APPROPRIATE STYLE**

3 a) Which features of story writing does the highlighter on page 54 identify? One has been done for you.

Features of story writing

★ Carefully choosing words to create atmosphere.

★ Using phrases that help to control pace (speed).

★ Using uninteresting background detail.

★ Showing off language skills through interesting images.   **blue**

b) Tick the features that are good to use.

c) Which of these language areas do you most need to improve?

> **TIP** ★ A main difference between Level 5 and Level 6 is often the care with which details and words are chosen. Taking out words and sentences that are not interesting can help a piece of writing.

4 Rewrite the section on page 54 highlighted in grey. It is not a very interesting part of the story, so just keep it short.

_____
_____
_____

5 a) Continue text **A** to the point where the person discovers what they are looking for.

> **TIP** ★ Use as much interesting language as you can – show off!

b) Review your work using the highlighters to identify:
   ★ precise words used for description;
   ★ phrases that control pace;
   ★ 'show-off' style images (like 'dazzled by darkness').

c) Write a list of useful techniques for story writing.

55

LEVEL 5–6 WRITING SKILLS

Improve your writing to review

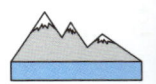

Level 5 writers explain opinions clearly and politely.
Level 6 writers explain opinions in detail, using an appropriate tone.

1 Imagine this report has appeared in your local newspaper. Read it carefully.

Election vote winner?

Voters will be making their minds up at next month's local elections. The Independent Party candidate, Mary Forest, hopes she has a vote winner with her idea of 'Teenage Service'.

What it involves

She plans to send squads of young people to clear up litter, clean ponds, create nature areas and help to install new playground equipment. She also thinks many pensioners would welcome some help to clear up their gardens.

Summer projects

She proposes that all 13–18-year-olds should spend two weeks of every summer term involved in various projects to improve the local environment and community. She believes that both teenagers and the community would benefit from her idea.

Send us your views

This newspaper would like to gather local feeling on the proposal. We invite you to set out your views. Send them to us and the most interesting contribution will appear in next week's edition of this paper.

2 The newspaper editor is looking at some comments. Tick the two that would be suitable to appear in the paper.

★ I'm not giving up my time. Mary Forest is obviously mad … ☐

★ I'm not old enough to vote but I'm old enough to have my say about … ☐

★ I already help my gran out, so that's it as far as I'm … ☐

★ I wonder if Mary Forest has actually asked teenagers what they think about … ☐

★ She should be locked up … ☐

TIP ★ A quick plan makes sure you include the most important points. Then, when you are writing, you can focus on your language.

LEVEL 5–6 USING AN APPROPRIATE STYLE

3 Now set out your view on Mary Forest's proposals. Make sure your readers can follow your ideas.

> **TIP** ★ Remember why you're writing and that your comments could appear in public. You need to show you are giving serious thought to the issue.

The opening sentences of your paragraphs can be helpful signposts. They don't have to be boring. You might want to make your reader sit up and take notice.

> If Mrs Forest asked for volunteers instead of ordering us around, she might be surprised at how many of us are interested in improving the environment …

> Putting up playground equipment is a skilled job, not one for a bunch of amateurs. If I were a parent, I'd want to know my kids were safe …

Next, try to create interesting starts for paragraphs about any three of these topics.
- ★ Litter clearing
- ★ Tidying pensioners' gardens
- ★ Pond cleaning
- ★ What would happen if pupils refused to turn up
- ★ Not having enough time for school exams

To present your views convincingly, you'll need to build up your sentences. Use connectives in the middle or at the start of sentences to help, e.g.:

I agree with your wish to improve the community. You are going about it in the wrong way.

▼ *Becomes*

I agree with your wish to improve the community although you are going about it in the wrong way.

▼ *Or*

Although I agree with your wish to improve the community, you are going about it in the wrong way.

_____ _____ _____
_____ _____ _____
_____ _____ _____
_____ _____ _____

> **TIP** ★ Remember: there are many useful connectives, e.g. *if, as, because, until, when, except, since, where, even if, however, on the other hand*. Try to use some when you write your response.

LEVEL 5–6 WRITING SKILLS

How to tackle the writing task

It's the start of the test: read the writing task carefully and don't panic! Before you start writing you need the answer to FOUR questions.

> **WHO is the WRITER?** Are you writing as yourself, or as another person?
> **WHO is the READER?** Are you writing this for anyone in particular (apart from the examiner, of course)?
> **WHAT FORM of writing is it?** Is it a letter? A report? A story? Or something else?
> **WHAT is its PURPOSE?** Is it to inform? To describe? To persuade? Or something else?

The answers to these four questions are always in the task: LOOK for them. Sometimes you have to work it out from clues.

These four things – WRITER, READER, FORM and PURPOSE – will have a big impact on what and how you write.

★ They will affect your ideas and the sort of detail you include.
★ They will affect the words and phrases you choose.
★ They will affect how you organise your ideas.
★ They will affect your tone (the sort of voice you use – polite, friendly, etc.).

It's just like when we talk – we change the tone, the words we use and what we say according to **who** we are, **who** we are speaking to and **why** we are talking.

Think of these writers:

A A businesswoman writes a letter to her bank to explain why she needs a loan and to persuade them to lend her some money.

B A teenage boy writes an email to his best friend to tell him what was good and bad about a rock festival he went to.

C A journalist writes a report for a newsaper about a heroic act.

D A novelist writes the opening chapter of a novel to send to a publisher.

Ask yourself the four questions: **WRITER? READER? FORM? PURPOSE?** for the four writers, **A, B, C, D**. In some cases you have to work out the answer for yourself. Fill in this table with the answers.

	Who is the writer?	Who is the reader?	What is the form?	What is the purpose?
A				
B				
C				
D				

All writers have to make their writing interesting for the reader. They all have to include details and develop their ideas. But there will be some differences.

Test yourself: practice writing tasks
Longer writing task

> **TIP** ★ **Quality** is better than **quantity**!

Work on your own. You have 45 minutes for the longer writing task in your Key Stage 3 writing test. Use about 10 minutes for planning. Allow five minutes for making changes at the end.

imagine, entertain, explore

Education International

Dear student

You have been invited to represent your school in an international writing competition.

Make one of your best school memories come alive through your writing.

Yours faithfully

Headteacher

Write your story, using the planning sheet on page 60 to help you organise your writing.

Shorter writing task

You have 30 minutes for the shorter writing task in your Key Stage 3 writing test.

> **TIP** ★ Use about five minutes for planning. Allow five minutes for making changes at the end.

inform, explain, describe

Local Heroes

You see this notice in your local newspaper:

We want to know who our local heroes are. The kind of people who make your day a little better in some way. It could be a cheery shop worker, a helpful lollipop lady or the person who serves you in the chip shop. Tell us about them and why they should win a Community Reward.
Send your entries to: The Editor, Local News …

Write a brief letter describing your favourite local character.

LEVEL 5–6

WRITING SKILLS

Planning sheet for longer writing task

Make notes about your ideas.

My favourite memory

How I will organise my writing to interest my readers

Interesting words and phrases I will use

LEVEL 5–6   TEST YOURSELF: PRACTICE WRITING TASKS

Self-assessment sheet

★ Look at the descriptions in the Level 6 section of the table.

★ In your work, find examples of the descriptions in the table.

★ Highlight the description in the table and an example in your work.

★ If you have at least ten of the Level 6 descriptions highlighted, you have achieved Level 6.

★ In a different colour, highlight what you still need to improve.

Level	Sentence structure	Punctuation	Paragraph organisation	Organisation inside paragraphs	Effect on the reader
6	I am beginning to choose my language for its effect on the reader, eg.: I use longer sentences when I want to show relationships between ideas; I use short sentences for emphasis or drama when needed; I use different types of words to open sentences, e.g. ___ing words, ___ly words, time (*Five days later* …).	Most of my punctuation is correct. I can use commas, instead of brackets, for 'extra' information in sentences. I can sometimes use semi-colons correctly when they are required.	I can use paragraphs of different lengths to help my reader, or to create an effect. My opening paragraph clearly introduces ideas that I will follow up later in the writing. I use a range of connecting words to link my paragraphs, e.g. *Consequently …, Soon after this …, In addition …* etc.	My paragraphs have a clear theme, which is developed across a number of sentences. Sometimes I delay giving information to my reader to create a better effect. I give my reader clear signals about the direction of the writing, e.g. *In the end … In contrast … Overall …*, etc.	I write in a style that suits the format of a story or a description. I help my reader to get involved in my writing by using interesting and precise details. I try to use some ambitious language to interest my reader, e.g. *dazzling darkness, perfect candidate.*
5	I use a range of different sentence types. I use different openings for my sentences, e.g. *I think …The train stopped … If …* I use connectives such as *although, while* and *even if* to link ideas in my sentences. I can use some 'strings of verbs' accurately, e.g. *I will be able to visit … He could have jumped …*	The ends of my sentences are correctly punctuated. When I use speech punctuation, I place the commas correctly. I use commas to mark clauses for sentences beginning with *Although …, Because …, If …, When …,* etc.	The order of my paragraphs is logical, e.g. most important to least important points/clear time sequence. My conclusion has links to my introduction or the main idea of the text, e.g. by summarising in an argument or tying up loose ends in a story.	My paragraphs have a main point and a number of 'smaller points' on the same topic. My paragraphs openings give clear signals to the reader, e.g. a topic sentence or *Later*, etc.	I develop my ideas across a number of sentences. I use a range of interesting words that make my ideas clear, e.g. *worthwhile, recommend, suitable.* I recognise my reader by using words that suit the task, e.g. *to be polite, to persuade.*

ANSWERS

Reading skills

Pages 10–11: Finding information and evidence in a text (1)

1   a) False (line to 'largest tribe')   b) False (line to 'live almost entirely')   c) flat – False (line to 'rolling hills'), ugly – False (line to 'stunning landscape'), desert – False (line to 'lush pasture')
2   a) Mtele knew the area. The ranger was experienced and had a gun.
    b) Mears was new to area/Mears was not local/Mtele was used to the conditions.
3   protection from animals; gives light; gives heat; gives comfort; a signal for other travellers

Pages 12–13: Finding information and evidence in a text (2)

2   Camp site C
3   a) Instruction B
3   b) 1–C; 2–B; 3–E; 4–D; 5–A; 6–F

Pages 14–15: What does the writer mean but not tell you directly? (1)

1   a) Yes; No
2   a) *Any two of:* 'concentrated entirely', 'without spilling a drop', 'exactly equal numbers', 'precise centre', 'carried it so carefully'
    b)–c) *Check with your teacher.*
3   *Check with your teacher.*

Pages 16–17: What does the writer mean but not tell you directly? (2)

1   C, B, A, E, F, D
2–4   *Check with your teacher.*

Pages 18–19: Commenting on the organisation of a text (1)

1   'You're only a few clicks away from providing the support that could change someone's life'; 'Giving regularly really is the best way to support Oxfam'; 'What can you buy for 16p a day?'
2   a) Level 5   b) Level 6   c) Level 5   d) Level 6
3   The biggest figure comes first because the writer wants to highlight that most of the money donated is spent helping people.

Pages 20–21: Commenting on the organisation of a text (2)

1   a) 'Uncle took me to market and sold me'
    b) They are both about Lu Si-yan being taken to the market.
    c) To shock and interest the reader.
2   para 2–D, B; para 3–A, C
3   Increases tension as reader is more alert or suspicious of other characters' actions.
4   *Sample answer:*
    1 introduces idea/suggests a problem
    2 describes conditions at sea
    3 gives family background
    4 shows how bleak home is
5   *Sample answer:*
    Writer unveils a little information in each paragraph to interest reader and to build a picture of the boy's life. This provides the reader with enough information to *know* that he will go to sea whether his father wants him to or not.

Pages 22–23: Commenting on how a writer uses language for effect (1)

1   a) repetition – 'a man'; a list – 'soaked in water, and smothered in mud, and lamed by stones, and cut by flints, and stung by nettles, and torn by briars'/'who limped, and shivered and glared and growled; alliteration – 'glared and growled'/'soaked' and 'smothered'
    b) To make the man seem frightening a bit like an animal.
    c) circle 'glared and growled'
    d) *Check with your teacher.*
2   b)–d) *Check with your teacher.*

Pages 24–25: Commenting on how a writer uses language for effect (2)

1   a) yellow   b) green   c)/d) light/interesting   e)/f) slower/clumsier
2   *Check with your teacher.*

Pages 26–27: Understanding the writer's viewpoint and the overall effect of the text (1)

1   a) *Check your answer with your teacher.*
    b) correct   c) Level 5
2   a)–e) True
3–5   *Check with your teacher.*

Pages 28–29: Understanding the writer's viewpoint and the overall effect of the text (2)

2   a) short   b) describes   c) real   d) last   e) impression
3   a) negative   b) 'sharp-faced'/'tight little mouth'/'curved downwards'
    c) *Check with your teacher.*
4   *Check with your teacher.*

Test yourself: practice reading tests

Reading test 1: Story Maker

Page 31: Text A

1   a) True   b) True   c) False   d) False
2   That Amir was the more powerful one in the relationship/He could read, but Hassan could not.
3   The pause shows Amir's shock, surprise. Just saying it shows a pause does not show what the effect is.

ANSWERS

4 Suggests powerful and sudden thoughts/could be a pleasant or unpleasant experience depending on interpretation of fireworks.
5 Answer may refer to:
   • arrogance/a bit spiteful/ready to tease Hassan;
   • surprise/enjoyment of Hassan's praise;
   • happy but puzzled or wondering about his story-telling skill.
   With suitable quotations.
   Check your answer with a teacher.

Page 33: Text B
6 **a)** False **b)** False **c)** True **d)** False
7 He expected some changes and was pleased with them.
8 At least 2 of the following explained: *proud/fond/familiar with/grateful for*
   With suitable quotations.
9 *Check with your teacher.*

Reading test 2: Attack!
Page 35: Text A
1 1–E; 2–B; 3–C; 4–D; 5–A; 6–F
2 equal distance apart; no advantage from wind; no advantage from light
3 Crowd were: silent; excited, expectant, waiting.
4 'like a dark flame' – the speed and danger of the net; 'licked' – the flickering/sweeping movement of the net, like the tongue of some dangerous beast
5 *Check with your teacher.*

Page 37: Text B
6 first half: confident/in control/relaxed/the hunter
   second half: panic/loss of control/becomes the hunted
7 Needed air to breathe.
8 *Any two from:* painful/intense memory; remain with him like a scar; never be able to forget it
9 *Check with your teacher.*

Writing skills
Pages 40–41: Using a wider range of connectives
1 **a)** when **b)** as **c)** before/after **d)** although
2 as/before/when/after/although
3 **a)** When **b)** Even though
4 *Check with your teacher.*

Pages 42–43: Adding detail with adjectives
1–5 *Check with your teacher.*

Pages 44–45: Adding detail with adverbial phrases
1 *Check with your teacher.*
2 **a)** with a quick wipe of his eyes
   b) with surprise
   c) with a defiant glare
3 *Check with your teacher.*

Pages 46–47: Using a full range of punctuation
2 The interview had been arranged for 10 o'clock and I arrived at reception 10 minutes early. (;) I wanted to make a good impression. My father, who had been in the army for 20 years, had drummed into me the importance of being on time. 'On time means you're on the ball,' he used to say to me. It was a lesson I had never forgotten. (;) It served me well that day. (;) If I hadn't have been early, I wouldn't have seen the man who staggered out of the lift. He was holding a blood-stained handkerchief to his face and looked as if he was about to faint. A strange thought crossed my mind. Was he on the interview list before me? I offered to help him but he left the building muttering, 'No job's worth that.' When I looked at my watch, I saw my turn had come.

3 **A** The semi-colons could go in a number of places. It depends which sentences you want to show the reader are linked.
   B 'It all began one year ago. In those 12 months he had changed so much.'
4 *Check with your teacher.*

Pages 48–49: Improve the organisation of your writing
1

Words that give order to instructions	Words that show time in a story	Words that link ideas in an argument
finally, *next*, *first*, *after this*	*meanwhile*, *eventually*, *soon*, *afterwards*, *next*	*however*, *in addition*, *finally*

2–3 *Check with your teacher.*

Pages 50–51: Improve your informative writing
1–3 *Check with your teacher.*

Pages 52–53: Improve your persuasive writing
1 **a), b)** using a quotation – 'We hold these truths to be self-evident, that all men are created equal' (to give authority to your idea)

giving a positive idea – 'will be transformed into an oasis of freedom and justice' (to show your idea will be good)

repeating a phrase – 'I have a dream' (to build an impression in your audience's mind

giving a personal example – 'my four little children' (to make your idea seem real or familiar to people)

giving a negative example – 'the state of Mississippi, a state sweltering with the heat of injustice, sweltering with the heat of oppression' (to show that things are not good now)

finishing with a short, dramatic point – 'I have a *dream* today!' (so that people will remember your idea)

ANSWERS

2–3 *Check with your teacher.*

Pages 54–55: Improve your imaginative writing

2 **a)** story A

b) *Check with your teacher.*

3 **a), b)** yellow – carefully choosing words to create atmosphere; green – to control pace (speed); grey – using uninteresting background detail; blue – showing off language skills

c) *Check with your teacher.*

4–5 *Check with your teacher.*

Pages 56–57: Improve your writing to review

2 'I'm not old enough to vote but I'm old enough to have my say about …';
'I wonder if Mary Forest has actually asked teenagers what they think about …'

3 *Check with your teacher.*

Page 58: How to tackle the writing task

If you have given more detail than this, so much the better. The important thing is that you have thought about the differences between different types of writing.

	Who is the writer?	Who is the reader?	What is the form?	What is the purpose?
A	business woman	Bank manager, an experienced profesional in money matters.	formal letter	To give information about the project/to persuade the manager to lend money
B	teenage boy	Best friend, probably teenage boy.	email	To describe/give information about a festival/to review bands or songs/to entertain or amuse a friend
C	journalist	People, male and female, of all ages around the country	newspaper report	To give factual information about the event/to hold the reader's interest
D	novelist	Readers of all ages, male and female.	novel	To entertain readers/to use imagination and invent/to make readers feel part of an imagined situation/to describe places, events or people

Test yourself: practice writing tasks

Page 59: Longer writing task
Check your answers with your teacher.

Page 59: Shorter writing task
Check your answers with your teacher.